The story of the Spanish and Portuguese Jews of the West Indies tells the history of the Western Hemisphere. Did you know that:

- The first European commercial tobacco grower was Luis de Torres, the interpreter in Columbus' crew. He was baptized dockside in 1492 just before they left Spain, so he would be allowed to sail on the Niña.

- Jews in Surinam were given religious freedom in 1652.

- In 1781, when British forces conquered the Dutch island of St. Eustatius, they singled out Jewish merchants for punishment, because of their assistance to the American colonies during the Revolutionary War.

- Until 1840, the only ordained rabbis in the Western Hemisphere were those in the West Indies.

The Dutch, British, Spanish, French and Danish islands of the Caribbean are rich in Jewish history.

Read on…

D0912008

Praise for first edition of
500 Years in the Jewish Caribbean

This is a book that makes history come alive. To walk in the footsteps of some of our forbearers evokes a fascination, rare indeed... a magnificent tapestry which Ezratty has woven.
- **Rabbi Bernard M. Zlotowitz**
  The Bulletin, New York Board of rabbis

A splendid job. You have provided a helpful resource for the Jewish traveler to the Caribbean and for those who love interesting sidebars to history.
- **Rabbi Bradd Boxman**
  United Jewish Center, Danbury, CT.

Your survey of life on the various islands depicts the integral role of Sephardim in the economic and cultural development on the Dutch, British, French and Spanish possessions.
- **Dr. M. Mitchell Serls, Director**
  Sephardic Community Programs, Yeshiva University

Your book is very interesting and informative about our contribution to the new world... comprehensive and all encompassing.
- **Rabbi Asher Murciano**
  Sephardic Jewish Center of Forest Hills, New York

Congratulations on an excellent book.
- **Bruce Young Candelaria**
  Executive Director, Hispanic-American Chamber of Commerce, Boston, MA.

More praise for first edition of
<u>500 Years in the Jewish Caribbean</u>

Il s'agit ici d'une etude systématique de l'implantation de juifs dans toutes les iles Caraibes, quie l'auteur n'a cessé de visiter et parcourir une par une depuis trente ans. Il nous livre le fruit de son travail de recherché et mémoire. S'il sous-titre son livre The Spanish and Portuguese Jews in the West Indies c'est qu'il se revendique lui meme fierement comme Sépharade...

- **La Lettre Sepharade**
  French edition

A valuable historical and tourist guide of our heritage in the Caribbean. Every island that ever had a Sephardic presence is carefully described and analyzed by this well-traveled detective of our heritage.

- **Erensia Sefardi/Sephardic Heritage**
  Connecticut

Author Harry A. Ezratty has written a fine book.

- **Lashon**
  Los Angeles

A delightful survey and overview, almost a travel guide, full of little-known facts and information about the history of those Sephardic Jews who escaped the Inqisition and lived in the West Indies. With his (Ezratty's) guidance, we make a trip through Curacao then visit St. Eustatius, St. Maarten, Jamaica, Nevis, Barbados, Trinidad, Martinique and Haiti.

- **Israel Cohen**
  <u>Ke Haber?/What's Happening,</u>
  Palm Beach County, Florida.

More praise for first edition of
<u>500 Years in the Jewish Caribbean</u>

A remarkable book – fascinating and very informative. A book well worth owning and especially for the Judaica philatelic collector.
- **Bea Stadtler**
  <u>The Israel Philatelist.</u>

Este libro konta en forma muy breve la istoria de los konversos ke yegaron a toda la rejoin de los Caribes, donde pudieron bivir kon mas seguridad ke en los otros paizes de las Amerikas, kreando mismo en siertos lugares komunitaes onde podian pratikar aviertamente la relijion djudia, kan sus sinagogas l simeterios, sus rabinos, hazanim l moalim, etc.
- **<u>Sepharade</u>**

I enjoyed your book very much and recited excerpts during our Shabbat services.
- **Dr. E. F. Einhorn**
  Polish Chamber of Commerce, Asia and Pacific Region.

People who use our library will find this book meaningful and useful.
- **Rabbi David A. Lyon**
  Cong. *Shaarey Zedek,* East Lansing, Michigan

Your opus is mighty impressive.
- **Rabbi Jack Stern**
  Massachusetts

I read it cover to cover and found it very interesting.
- **Judge Raymond L. Acosta**
  U.S. District Court for the District of Puerto Rico

Excellent book! Easily readable and interesting subject matter.
- **Judge Richard D. Huttner**
- New York Supreme Court

500 Years in the Jewish Caribbean

The Spanish and Portuguese Jews in the West Indies

Harry A. Ezratty

Read Street Publishing
Baltimore Maryland

www.readstreetpublishing.com

500 Years in the Jewish Caribbean: The Spanish
and Portuguese Jews in the West Indies

By Harry A. Ezratty
ISBN: 978-0-942929-49-2
Copyright © 1997, revised 2002, 2020

Read Street Publishing
133 West Read Street, Baltimore, MD 21201
www.readstreetpublishing.com
editor@readstreetpublishing.com

Cover: St. Thomas Jewish Cemetery at Savan; c. 1971
Cover Design: Alan Hirsch
Interior Design: Richard Gottesman, Sutileza Graphics

Photographs were taken by and are the property of the
author, except for the photo of the St. Thomas Synagogue,
which was provided by Rabbi Bradd Boxman, and photo
of Temple *Beth Shalom* in Puerto Rico, which was taken by
Alan Hirsch.

BOOKS BY HARRY EZRATTY

Non Fiction

How to Qualify for Multi-Bar Practice

The Seaman's Handbook of Rights

How to Collect and Protect Works of Art

Jews in the New World Trilogy
      Vol. 1: 500 Years in the Jewish Caribbean:
            The Spanish and Portuguese Jews in the West Indies
      Vol. 2: They Led the Way: The Creators of Jewish America
      Vol. 3: The Builders: Jews and the Growth of America

Baltimore, A City Divided: the Pratt Street Riot

Fiction

The Dan Nikolas Esq., series:
      False Passage
      Flags of Convenience

The Noah Pardo Series:
      The Bureau of Military Information
      The 20-Cent Quarters (in preparation)

DEDICATION

This book is dedicated to my father Joseph (Pepo) Ezratty, (1904-1998) whose family reluctantly left Spain in 1492, finally settling in the Ottoman Empire, in the city of Salonica. For more than 400 years, each male born into the family was duly registered with the Spanish consul of that city. The practice stopped when Pop moved to America, but he always took great care to instruct me in my Jewish and Sephardic heritage.

ACKNOWLEDGEMENTS

I thank Gloria Sanchez for her dedication in the preparation of the first edition of this book (she tells me she learned much about the Jewish people while in front of her computer); Alan Hirsch for designing an eye-catching and pertinent cover; Richard Gottesman of Sutileza Graphics for his superior design work on the interior of this latest edition, and Michelle Ezratty Murphy for her assistance with photos.

Many thanks, too, to Barbara Tasch Ezratty, my wife and editor. As a professional writer, she led me through many parts of the book with kindness and understanding. Her patience and encouragement made my work much easier.

And finally, thanks to all the people I've met and spoken with throughout the islands, whose names may not appear in the book but who, for more than four decades, have helped me increase my knowledge of the Jewish Caribbean.

CONTENTS

CONTENTS

INTRODUCTION

In the fall of 1991, the adult education chairperson of Temple *Beth Shalom* in San Juan, Puerto Rico asked me to prepare a program celebrating the role of the Jews in Caribbean history. The project was scheduled for 1992, in time for celebrations surrounding the discovery of the New World by Christopher Columbus 500 years earlier.

I mounted photographs and documents of Jewish life covering those 500 years, highlighting islands in the West Indies in which Jewish communities once flourished or still thrive. Accompanying the exhibit was my 20-page pamphlet, "500 Years in the Jewish Caribbean." I also lectured on the topic. To prepare all of this, I catalogued the photographs, documents, pamphlets, letters, books, newspaper and magazine articles concerning West Indian Jewry in my personal collection, as well as notes of conversations held with residents of the Caribbean over a 30-year period.

I have always been fascinated with the impact a small band of Sephardim (Jews of Spanish and Portuguese origin) made on the Americas from the 17th to 19th centuries. The history of their sojourn in the Caribbean Basin honors the Jewish people, for they paved the way for freedoms now taken for granted by all Jews of the Western Hemisphere.

Processing all this information reaffirmed for me certain facts: Caribbean Sephardim, from Colonial times to the end of the 19th Century, were a close-knit group. Their common languages were Portuguese, Hebrew, Spanish and English. They maintained solid business and family contacts throughout the islands, even to the American mainland. These connections helped them in business and kept their bloodlines going for many generations. They knew no political boundaries, moving back and forth between English, French, Dutch and Danish islands and the colonial American mainland as easily as we travel by jet today.

Finally, history tells us that from the beginning of their arrival in the Caribbean, Jews fought to gain a significant degree of liberty and religious freedom. To be sure, they were saddled with civil disabilities by their governments. Early in their Caribbean experience, they lobbied governments to be allowed to own land, farm, sit on juries, vote and bear arms to defend their homes and property.

Most of these rights and obligations were then unknown to European Jews, who were only just emerging from medieval political strictures. In the Caribbean, Moses Delgado won the vote for Jamaican Jews; Campoe Sabbatha led the British navy against the Spaniards, and was instrumental in freeing his fellow *Marranos* from Spanish-dominated Jamaica; and Captain Isaac Pinto in Surinam led an intrepid militia of Jewish plantation owners, defending their homes against pirates, Indians, slave revolts and the neighboring French. More than one writer has said these Sephardim were the world's first modern Jews.

Caribbean Jews voted earlier than their European cousins and, having won these rights, quickly jumped into the political, social and commercial life of their islands. So integrated were they that there have been few examples of anti-Semitism in the Caribbean. No West Indian government ever passed an anti-Jewish law following the infamous French *Code Noir* of 1685. (See the sections on Martinique and Guadeloupe for a discussion of the *Code Noir*.)

Here, then, is the book that developed from my earlier writings on the subject. It is intended to give readers an overview of the essence of the remarkable and exiting 500 year experience of Jews in the Caribbean.

In writing this introduction, I was reminded of when I took my children back to my old neighborhood, to show them where I grew up; where the movie houses and restaurants once were, the streets I walked and played on; the synagogue I went to, the house I lived in and the school where I studied. The children saw only run-down streets and buildings. The restaurants are no longer there; the schoolhouse was razed year earlier; the synagogue is now a Baptist temple. Only a few of the old buildings and businesses remained, still dedicated to their old functions. They are islands in a sea of change.

From the 17th to the 19 centuries, the Caribbean was a Jewish neighborhood. It has since changed. Sometimes a building still remains in use after hundreds of years but, mostly, the buildings and other sites have fallen into disuse. Why should an old Jewish neighborhood in the Caribbean be different from one in New York, Chicago, Los Angeles or Detroit?

Read further and you will learn what the "old neighborhood" was like and meet the people who once lived there. You'll also meet the people who remained.

Harry A. Ezratty
San Juan, Puerto Rico
1997

COMMENTS ON THIS EDITION

Reader reaction to the publication of this book's first edition was interesting. Puerto Rican colleagues whom I have known for decades, related that they had been told by grandparents and great-grandparents that they were Jewish, or that a Jewish thread ran through their lineage. Their comments were always positive. I felt an affirmation on their part that we shared a common Hispanic history.

One caller, a member of the Dominguez Wolff family of Puerto Rico, related an interesting story, one I never would have documented from available records.

His great-grandfather, a Wolff from St. Thomas, married his great-grandmother, a De Castro from that same island. Both families were well-known and distinguished members of the St. Thomas Jewish community. In 1833, a Wolff served as president of the St. Thomas congregation and contributed $300 to the construction of the island's historic synagogue.[1]

Fifty years later, during the last years of the Spanish colonial period, the Wolffs intended to establish a plantation on the island of Puerto Rico. They entered Puerto Rico through the satellite island of Vieques, off the main coast. Vieques was sparsely populated. There would have been a minimum presence of Spanish officialdom and security present.

---

[1] In "A Short History of the Hebrew Congregation of St. Thomas", p. 11. An earlier member of the Wolff family appears as president of the Jewish Congregation at St. Thomas. He is listed as giving, in 1833, the largest cash contribution towards the reconstruction of the now historic synagogue. Wolffs lived on several islands in the Caribbean, including St. Eustatius. In Emmanuel, I. & S., A History of the Jews of the Netherlands Antilles,, p. 105, Emmanuel notes the marriage of Mozes Wolff of Breslof, Germany to Rebecca Robles in 1794. The couple later moved to St. Thomas. Also, J. Margolinsky in his monograph "299 Epitaphs on the Jewish Cemetery in St. Thomas, W.I.", notes the headstones of 10 Wolffs in St. Thomas' Altona cemetery.

In order to buy land in the Spanish colony of Puerto Rico, the Wolffs were required to affirm they were Catholics. There was probably little scrutiny or concern for the truth or falsity of such an undertaking. But had they not done so, under Spanish law the Wolffs could not legally buy or own land in Puerto Rico. The descendants of the Wolffs living in Puerto Rico today are all Catholic.

Members of the Bravo family, also of Puerto Rico, lay claim to Jewish descent. This knowledge has been passed down through generations.

Through a mutual friend, I made contact with Jill Tattersall, an historian in Tortola, British Virgin Islands. She maintains that there are no records of any existing Jewish cemeteries, synagogues or other communal structures on these islands. There were, however, Jews living in Tortola by the middle of the 17th Century. There is documentation verifying the presence of Sephardic bankers during this period and evidence of them later being driven off by marauding Spaniards. Most refugees sought safety in nearby St. Thomas, or Dutch St. Eustatius.

Ms. Tattersall advises that one Abraham Mendes Bellisario was known to be Jewish. He was a leading resident of Tortola and a respected Road Town merchant. He must have been an outstanding citizen: in 1814, he was appointed Marshall of the Court of Vice-Admiralty, an important English tribunal of the time, especially in the West Indies where shipping was of great importance.

At the request of his descendants, she tried unsuccessfully to located Bellisario's grave, and those of other Jews who may have lived on this English island colony.[2]

A review of registered graves in the Jewish cemeteries of Barbados and St. Thomas reveals several Mendes Belisario or Belisarios buried there. And a Henry Mendes Belisario shows up as a bridegroom in 1862 in the Curaçao Marriage Register.

---

[2] Letter from Jill Tattersall, Roadtown, Tortola, British Virgin Islands. 1998

Differences in spelling should be of no importance. The 1800s was an age in which spelling was not a refined art. So the Belisarios were well-known West Indian Jews who settled throughout the islands. They followed the traditions of many other Jewish families who could point to relatives across the Caribbean.

Further research into Jamaican Jewry reveals that the National Artist for that nation, Isaac Mendes Belisario, was a member of the Jewish community. He was famous for painting Jamaican Blacks when they were emerging from slavery in the mid-1800s, with compassion, wit and understanding.[3]

I learned about Mendes Belisario through a slim volume called, "The Spanish and Portuguese Jews in the Postage Stamps," by Mordechai Arbell. This interesting book is printed in three languages, Hebrew, French and Ladino, the latter being the language of the Sephardic Diaspora.

Arbell, an Israeli diplomat, is knowledgeable about the region's Jewry. In his book, I read of Dr. Juan Lindo, jurist, educator and president of both El Salvador (1842-42) and then, amazingly of Honduras from 1847-1852.[4]

Lindo was a descendant of Sephardim, as was Moises F. Da Costa Gomez, one of modern Curaçao's great leaders. Another Caribbean educator and political leader who has West Indian Sephardic roots is Pedro Henriquez Urena, a past president of the Dominican Republic.[5]

---

[3] Arbell, The Spanish and Portuguese Jews in the Postage Stamps, p. 30. Mendes Belisario also painted a famous watercolor of London's Spanish and Portuguese synagogue. See Roth, The Life of Manasseh Ben Israel. Jewish Publication Soc., Philadelphia. 1945. p. 49.

[4] Ibid. p. 11

[5] Ibid. p. 47

Another family from Curaçao, the Shalom Delvalles, was to later have the honor of seeing one of their descendants, Max Shalom Delvalle, become the first Jewish president of Panama. [6]

A grand picture emerges, which by itself could be the subject of another book: the contemporary impact of West Indian Sephardim across their region. The story would be one of Jews and non-Jews now living throughout the islands who can trace their ancestry to early Sephardim and who are still making significant contributions to their island nations. The tale could extend to Central America, as Arbell has shown us, including Panama. While not, strictly speaking, West Indian, Central America has much Jewish history in common with the islands.

The most exciting new material of all is Cuba. Events for the Jewish community there now move with such speed, anything written today will have changed within a month. The changes are mostly all positive.

---

[6] Emmanuel, op. cit., Vol. II, p. 882, also "Interim Chief of State Installed in Panama", New York Times, April 8, 1968 (no byline.) Panama has had two Jewish presidents, the only country in the world apart from Israel with that distinction. (Eric Del Valle Maduro was president in 1987-1988). The basis of this information stems from a question posed to me by a friend, Rabbi Bernard Zlotowitz, who asked, "Was there ever a Jewish president in Panama?" He said when he was officiating at Yom Kippur services in Panama City as a visiting rabbi, he was eager to proceed with the traditional Kol Nidre service, since night was falling. "Wait," he was told more than once. "The president is not here yet." Finally, Panama's president Omar Torrijos entered the sanctuary, sat on a bench set aside for him, and the service began. After Kol Nidre, Torrijos left. Zlotowitz was puzzled. I explained that since Torrijos was not Jewish, the tradition of attendance must have started with his friend, Shalom Delvalle, Panama's first Jewish president, and Torrijos was continuing the tradition.

During those dark days of Cuba's isolation from the West, only three synagogues in all of Cuba remained open: Havana's *Shevet Ahim, Adath Israel,* and *La Patronata.* Since the publication of the first edition of this book, all three have seen increases in membership and activity. Bar Mitzvahs, weddings, circumcisions and other religious rites are now celebrated regularly. A cadre of volunteer rabbis, many Chasidic, from Canada, Mexico and elsewhere make regular visits to Cuba to service the blossoming community. American children, through their Jewish religious schools, make regular visits to Cuba, bringing food, pharmaceuticals and religious texts.[7]

From the 700 known Jews in 1991, the population had increased to 1,800 in 1997. There are reasons for the dramatic rise: gentile spouses of mixed marriages are converting; Jews who for decades maintained silence have come out into the open. And outside Havana, the city of Santiago de Cuba has reopened the doors of its synagogue after having been closed for over 20 years. A new synagogue is being built in Camaguey to accommodate that small Jewish community.[8]

It is not illogical to expect more Jews to soon surface with all of this increased and vigorous religious activity. As predicted in the first edition of this book, Cuba should soon become the Caribbean's leading Jewish community, providing its amazing rebirth continues.

---

[7] Conversations with Rabbi Gary Bretton-Granatoor, at the time rabbi of the Stephen Wise Free Synagogue, New York City, following his mission to Cuba in the year 2000.

[8] Conversations with and notes made by James and Sue Klau of Temple *Beth Shalom,* San Juan, Puerto Rico, following their mission to Cuba in the year 2001, together with the report prepared by them.

In this edition of my book, the bibliography has been expanded to include more newspaper and magazine articles, current books and conversations and letters. In addition, footnotes have been added to the text to enable readers to investigate this fascinating history in greater depth. And, of course, wherever necessary there have been updates of island life, including the addition of the Bahamas which, while geographically not in the Caribbean, are islands that have much in common with the West Indies.

Finally, having revisited many of these historic sites between the first and third editions and reading extensively about the conditions of others I could not get to, it is certain that these unique monuments of the Jewish people are in peril. Aside from environmental assaults, the existing Jewish communities which are in custody of these treasures, are so small they find it difficult to finance their preservation. On islands where there is no Jewish community, such as Nevis and St. Eustatius, the goodwill of governments who understand their custodial obligations cannot be depended upon indefinitely.

I hope this book will help in some ways to set before the public the condition of these historic monuments so a greater interest will help to preserve them for posterity.

Harry A. Ezratty
Baltimore, Maryland
2020

AUTHOR'S ADDENDUM

From 2015 to 2020, a series of natural disasters blew through the West Indies. Hurricane Joaquin in 2015 hovered over the Bahamas for 3 days, dropping unprecedented rain that washed away crops and created storm surges. In 2016, Matthew, another Category 5 hurricane devastated Haiti and the Bahamas. In 2017, Irma and Maria attacked St. Thomas, St. Croix and Puerto Rico, toppling trees, telephone and power lines. They caused massive mud slides, crushed houses and killed thousands of people.

More islands were affected by other hurricanes in 2019, which was also the year of multiple damaging earthquakes with forces high on the Richter Scale. Roads were destroyed and water supplies polluted. These consecutive events have been called the region's most serious natural disasters in recorded history.

The loss of life, housing, industry, schools, churches and synagogues – indeed, of entire infrastructures – has been responsible for an exodus of island citizens seeking safer locations. The resultant population decrease in the area is staggering.

Those who could stay were working, with government assistance in many cases, to improve their islands' infrastructures, until the 2019 Corona Virus Pandemic reached the Caribbean in early 2020 and halted all communal activities. Today, while scientists struggle to find relief, the world is practicing social distancing... and waiting.

Hopefully, when things return to an acceptable normalcy, rebuilding can continue and the Jews of the Caribbean will contribute to the effort, enabling the West Indies to once again be attractive to businesses, dependable to residents, and inviting to tourists. Everyone's goal is to regain the sun-filled tropical paradise that the Caribbean has been for so many centuries.

May 2020

1

A New Diaspora: Spain 1492

In 1391, the Archdeacon of Ecija harangued Seville's Christians until they became an anti-Jewish mob: this event had significance that extended far beyond its immediate importance.

The mob ran wild through the *Juderia* (Jewish quarter), leaping from Seville to all of Spain: to Cordova, Toledo and Barcelona, even to the island of Mallorca. Wherever it went, it attacked Jews, destroying their homes and looting their property. Vandals dragged Jewish families into the streets and handed them over to frenzied crowds.

It was the most concentrated anti-Jewish attack by Christians on the Iberian Peninsula. There had been anti-Jewish riots in Spain before, but none had been as ferocious, as wide-spread or as long-lasting as the countrywide turmoil of 1391.

From written accounts, the only way to escape alive was to submit to baptism: to accept Christianity. For many, it was a desperate act of self-preservation. Spanish Jews, also known as Sephardim from the Hebrew word for Iberia, had lived on the Iberian Peninsula in relative peace for centuries, never victim to the vicious anti-Semitic pressures their Central and Eastern European cousins lived with. Mob tactics of this sort were new to them. Perhaps Spanish Jews were not equipped to withstand these pressures: their reaction was to give in to the conversion demands.[1]

Over the next 100 years, many descendants of those who reluctantly accepted Christianity continued to practice Judaism in

---

[1] Roth, The Spanish Inquisition, p. 21

1

secret. But as outwardly professing Catholics, new social and economic opportunities were now legally open to them. Rising in power and influence throughout Spain, they were represented at court, in business and even in the Church. But despite their conversion, the perceived stigma of a Jewish past clung to them. They were derisively known as "New Christians," "*Conversos*," or "*Marranos*," the latter a degrading term meaning swine. It was a name Jews themselves would later use with pride.[2]

By the mid-15th Century, alarmed Christians sought to curb the power of the rising Marrano class by forcing their strict adherence to the principles of the Church. In 1480, Queen Isabella and King Ferdinand issued commissions, under authorization of a Papal Bull, permitting Spanish clerics to organize an Inquisition to detect and punish heretics within the Catholic Church. Punishment could be death or loss of property and public penance of the most humiliating sort. During this period, the Church was at least as powerful as the Crown and shared confiscated Jewish property with the state.[3]

Practicing Jews, however, were outside the Inquisition's grasp. It was no secret that they were helping New Christians. Within Marrano circles were relatives, friends and business associates who secretly clung to their old religion and Jews who sympathized with their difficult position.

It was an intolerable situation for the Church: the Inquisition had no jurisdiction over Jews. Tomas de Torquemada, an influential priest (himself possibly of Jewish antecedents) solved the problem: he proposed the expulsion of Jews from all of Spain.[4]

Expulsion would at once remove the support system which nourished *Marranos*; it would rid the country of Jews and would allow the confiscation and division of their properties between Church and Crown at a time when funds were needed to pay for Spain's war against the Arabs.

---

[2] Roth, <u>History of the Marranos</u>, p. 27-28

[3] Ibid. p. 44-52

[4] Amler, <u>Christopher Columbus' Jewish Roots</u> p. 111

By 1492, all political factors were in place for Torquemada's plan. The Spanish army destroyed the last Muslim enclave at Granada. Spain could now enlarge and secure its borders and unite all its separate kingdoms into one nation. Spain would be bound by language and religion. The Expulsion would forever rid Spain of Jews and Muslims.

The Crown signed the Expulsion Decree of 1492. Stripped of all Jewish support, New Christians were defenseless before the Inquisition. Practicing Jews fled west to Portugal or east to the Ottoman Empire. Others converted to Christianity in order to remain. The significant minority that fled to Portugal found sanctuary there to be brief. In 1497, Spain pressured Portugal to install its own Inquisition as part of the political price for the union of their royal houses in marriage.[5]

Portuguese Jews had no choices. King Manoel, aware that his Jewish subjects were valuable, would not allow them to leave and ordered they all be converted. Each and every Jew in Portugal who protested was dragged to the baptismal font and forcibly baptized.

Portuguese Jews were not like the Spanish Jews who had elected to remain in Spain: Portuguese Jews had no choice. Many remained Jews in secret.[6]

By the end of the 15th Century, there were no openly professing Jews on the Iberian Peninsula. Spain's Expulsion of 1492 and the 1497 Portuguese forced conversions dropped the curtain on more than 1,000 years of Hispanic Jewish life.

Simultaneous with the Decree of Expulsion, Christopher Columbus was authorized to sail west to contact Asian lands and rulers. His voyage opened a new chapter in Jewish history, one that would propel Jews to their greatest freedom.

To understand the Jewish role in Columbus' discovery of the New World, we must examine some New Christians in the Spanish Court and Jews whose scientific discoveries were to have a great influence on the Admiral:

---

[5] Roth, The Spanish Inquisition, p.2

[6] Ibid, p. 133

- Luis de Santangel, Gabriel Sanchez, and other descendants of converted Jews who were members of Ferdinand and Isabella's court, undertook to raise the necessary cash for Columbus' enterprise. Contrary to what children in elementary school have been taught, Isabela never pledged her jewels or anything else of value for that matter, to underwrite Columbus's voyages[7];
- Abraham Senior, a rabbi and Queen Isabella's long-time advisor, (who later converted in order to remain in Spain) also urged the Crown to back Columbus[8];
- The Crescas family, known as "the map Jews", whose charts and navigational instruments were used by Columbus.[9]
- Abraham Zacuto, one of the Iberian Peninsula's leading astronomers, a rabbi and a geographer who, in addition to refining the Astrolabe (a medieval wooden version of the sextant), also provided Columbus with his "Tables of Zacuto," a compendium of the movements of the sun, moon and planets.

By measuring the rising and setting of the sun and moon and the positions of important stars, the Tables were of great use to Columbus and later to Vasco de Gama. On one occasion, Zacuto's Tables predicted an eclipse, which saved Columbus' life during the year he was shipwrecked in Jamaica. He was able to correctly

---

[7] Amler, op. cit., p. 105-116

[8] Roth, History of the Marranos p. 8. Rabbi Abraham Senior was an intermediary in the marriage between Ferdinand and Isabela. After his conversion, he took the name Fernado Perez Coronel.

[9] Amler, op. cit., p. 25

predict the eclipse to hostile Caribbean natives who became docile, awed by what they believed to be his magical powers.[10]

Zacuto refused to convert and fled from Iberia to exile in North Africa and the Ottoman Empire, where he spent the remainder of his life teaching in obscurity at small schools and academies.[11]

At the close of the 15th Century, the world was a grim place for Jews. During the preceding 400 years, they had been expelled from every country in Western Europe, forbidden to return. Until 1492 and 1497, Spain and Portugal had been safe places. Now, Turkey and its conquered territories along the North African coast offered the only haven.

Scores of thousands of forcibly converted Jews were trapped in Spain and Portugal, their position intolerable. The Inquisition was tracking them down and swiftly eliminating all hidden traces of Judaism from Hispanic society.

It was Columbus' 'discovery' of a new world that gave Sephardim new hope and the greatest outlet for their talents and for religious liberty.

---

[10] Congress Monthly, Sept/Oct 1992, "Return to Toledo." Zacuto recorded his sad exile. He fled to Portugal where he helped Vasco da Gama, as he had for Columbus, with astronomical charts. He then fled Portugal for Tunis. The Inquisition followed him there, also. He moved to Damascus and then, Jerusalem. In his absence from Iberia, he wrote Sefer Yuhasin, the Book of Generations., a tale of the sweet and bitter history that befell the Jewish people.

[11] Roth, History of the Marranos, p. 54. See also Kayserling, Christopher Columbus and the Participation of the Jews in the Spanish and Portuguese Discoveries, pp. 46-51

2

100 Years of Hiding in the Caribbean

It is no small irony that Luis de Torres may have been the first European to walk upon the soil of the New World on October 12, 1492. He was not only a member of Columbus' crew, he was once Jewish.[1] His Hebrew name was Josef Ben Levi Ha I'vri (Joseph son of Levi the Hebrew.)

As a practicing Jew, de Torres would not have been permitted to live in any Spanish territory, let alone sail on the expedition of discovery. To leave Spain with the crew, de Torres had to accept Christianity before sailing. It is said he was baptized at the dock as the squadron was about to leave on what was to become one of the world's great voyages.

---

[1] Roth, History of the Marranos (HM), p. 272. Roth states that de Torres "was, as a matter of fact, the first European to set foot in the new land." Amler in Christopher Columbus' Jewish Roots (CCJR), states at p. 157 that de Torres went ashore with several men, including Martin Pinzon, second in command after Columbus. Who touched shore first is in my opinion an open question. Undoubtedly, de Torres was at least among the very first. Columbus himself failed to mention de Torres at this historic point in his journal: see Jane, Cecil (translator), The Journals of Christopher Columbus. Nor does Dr. Kayserling (Christopher Columbus and the Participation of the Jews in the Spanish and Portuguese Discoveries (CC) p. 93.) Certainly de Torres was at least one of the first as they went from island to island, for it was he who had been deputized to translate. What we do know is that de Torres became one of the first colonizers of Cuba; the first Jewish planter in the New World; and the first European commercial cultivator of tobacco. CC, p. 94-95; HM, p. 272; CCJR, p. 217.

De Torres signed on as ship's interpreter. Fluent in Hebrew, Aramaic and Arabic, it was expected that he would use these languages as the Admiral's voice before the rulers of the East.[2]

There may have been as many as four others in the crew who, like de Torres, were Jews who converted. At least two, Mestre Bernal, the flotilla's surgeon who was pursued by the Inquisition and whose wife was burned for heresy, and its doctor, Marco, have been documented as *Marranos*.[3] One of the Sanchez courtiers to the crown, also converted, served as Isabela's representative.

The enterprising de Torres, when he had no official duties in Cuba to keep him busy, soon became acquainted with the dried tobacco leaf that Cuban natives rolled, burned and inhaled with great pleasure. He remained in the Caribbean cultivating tobacco, one of the West Indies' first European colonists, the first in a long series of Jewish planters in the Caribbean.

For 100 years, Jews who sailed to the New World were forced to hide their true religion. That was the price exacted to escape the Inquisitions in Spain and Portugal. Discovery of this secret could mean death, as first the Spanish and then the Portuguese Inquisitions followed them across the Atlantic to the New World.

Jews in the Caribbean during the 1500s hid their true religion to escape torture, murder, or at the very least, confiscation of their property. The Crown became so alarmed at the number of New Christians seeking to colonize the New World, it issued edicts preventing them from doing so.[4]

In one of the most dramatic actions by the Inquisition in the New World, 40 members of the Carvajal family of Mexico, headed by the Governor of *Nuevo Leon*, Luis de Carvajal, were burned,

---

[2] Kayserling op. cit. p. 90. In 1658, Moses Nehemiah, a Sephardi from Barbados, brought the Caribbean tobacco culture to Virginia. "A Brief History of the Jewish Settlement in Barbados". [no author, no date.] Barbados Tourist Board, p. 9.

[3] Roth, History of the Marranos. P. 272. In fact, crewmember Alfonso de la Caballeria was a relative of Gabriel Sanchez, one of the *Marranos* at the royal court. According to Roth, another crew member, Alonso de la Calle, whose name ("of the street") indicates a name of Jewish origin, was probably also of Jewish descent.

[4] Amler, op. cit. p. 218

hung and hounded for over a decade for their religious beliefs. The Inquisition began its investigation of the family in 1589, alternately torturing and executing all of them until 1601, when Mariana de Carvajal, the last of the family, was strangled and then burned in a mass *Auto de Fe* (ritual burning of victims).[5]

Inquisition records reveal that secret Jews were discovered and tried in Hispaniola, Cuba, Puerto Rico, Trinidad, and Jamaica. The threat of discovery was paramount to all *Marranos* in the New World. But in 1588, a significant event occurred, one that would affect the entire Caribbean and the future of its Jewish presence.

Sir Frances Drake and his British privateers swept Spain's Armada from the English Channel. Helped by a violent storm, they sunk the Armada to the bottom of the Channel. Spanish sailors and ships washed ashore as far West as Ireland. Spain would never regain its naval strength and position as Europe's most powerful force in the Caribbean.

Without commanding sea power, Spain could no longer protect all her interests in the West Indies. Once the only colonial power in the Caribbean, she was now forced to focus on the larger islands of the Greater Antilles: Jamaica, Cuba, Hispaniola, Puerto Rico and, further to the south, Trinidad. There, the wealth of her colonies could be consolidated.

Spain's rivals, England, France, Holland and Denmark rushed in to fill the vacuum south of the Greater Antilles. By the 17th Century, Spain had lost control of every island south of Puerto Rico except Trinidad. In the Greater Antilles, she lost half of Hispaniola to the French, and Jamaica to the English. She finally surrendered Trinidad to Great Britain in 1795.

At the same time, the still-practicing secret Jews of Spain and Portugal were filtering out of the Iberian Peninsula. Some sailed east to the Ottoman Empire but most fled to safety in Holland, Germany, Denmark and later, England. During the 17th Century, these latter countries were leaders of the Protestant Revolution: they were outside the grasp of the Catholic Church and its Inquisition.

---

[5] Cohen, Sephardim in the Americas, p. 211

The Jews remaining in Spain and Portugal led double lives. If they traveled abroad with intent to return, they would assume Jewish identities and aliases. When they returned to Iberia, they resumed their Christian lives and names. Caribbean Sephardim would later use this device in a more complicated way. Dealing with Christians in Spanish America, they had to conceal their Jewishness. Sometimes it was prudent to behave as a Christian even among friends. The Inquisition relied on its agents and friends abroad to advise them of Spanish and Portuguese travelers maintaining contacts with overseas Jewish communities.

Sephardim often bore Hebrew first names like Elihu, Solomon, Isaac or Moshe. Families might have place names like Toledo, Sevillano or Murciano; trade names like Mercado, Herrera or Marino; or Arabic names, such as Abudiente or Abulafia.[6]

To emphasize a family's commitment to Judaism, a Hebrew family name might also be added. Thus the double family name, as in Cohen-Toledo, Levy-Rivera, or Aboab de Fonseca.

Completely new names were assumed and used when traveling or in business dealings, to prevent retaliation at home, should one be discovered practicing Judaism abroad. Moses Cohen might become Antonio Vaez Enriquez, or Joshua Toledo (Toledo was a common Jewish name) might become Juan de Madrid. The legendary Amsterdam ship owner, Manuel Rodrigues, was elsewhere known as Jacob Tirado. Tirado or Tyrado may also have assumed the names Guimes Lopez da Castro or Simon Lopez de Costa.[7]

Even children were drawn into the 'game.' One writer notes that when he asked some Marrano children their names, the countered with "which ones, our secret names or the ones we are known by?"[8]

---

[6] Karner, The Sephardics of Curaçao, p. 16-18

[7] Dubiez, The Sephardic Community of Amsterdam. My copy of this monograph has no pagination, no date of publication and no publisher. However, this work is cited in the bibliography of Curaçao's, "Our Snoa," at p. 79

[8] Ibid

One of the most intriguing examples of the use of double names may be found in the Barbados Jewish cemetery. On one bilingual gravestone, the name Joseph Jessurun Mendes is inscribed in Portuguese, the language used by the Jewish community in Barbados during the 17th and 18 Centuries. On the same stone, which would have been read by Mendes' Christian business and social associates in the Caribbean, his name is given in English as Lewis Dias. Mendes/Dias died in 1699. He was one of the founders of the Jewish community and was earlier active in the Recife synagogue in Brazil.[9]

Another more famous user of the double name was Gideon Rowland. Known as Rohiel Abundiente within the Jewish community of Nevis, Rowland also lived in Barbados and the American colonies. He retired to London a wealthy man and a pillar of Spanish-Jewish life. His son went on to become an advisor to the English crown. Later generations married into English royalty. Rowland's first wife's grave can be seen in Nevis. She was buried under the name of Batsheva Abundiente.[10]

It was in Holland during the late 16th and 17th centuries that Jews enjoyed their greatest freedom in Europe. At first, refugee Sephardim had a problem in Amsterdam. They arrived seemingly as Spanish Catholics. However, Holland had recently won independence from the Spaniards, renounced Catholicism, and accepted Protestantism. Hence, new Catholic refugees were not sympathetically received.

Early Jewish prayer groups in Amsterdam were broken up, the leaders arrested. But it soon became obvious to the Dutch that these new immigrants were what they claimed to be, "Roman

---

[9] Shilstone, <u>Monumental Inscriptions in the Jewish Synagogue of Bridgetown, Barbados</u>, p. x of the book's preface.

[10] Friedman, <u>Jewish Pioneers and Patriots</u>. Chapter 24 of Friedman's book, <u>The Gideons,</u> is a fascinating review of the Anglicization of a Portuguese Jewish family, the Gideon-Abundientes. Friedman traces the family from Europe to the Caribbean then colonial America, and finally back to England. Some of this family became titled members of the English establishment. See also Roth, <u>History of the Marranos</u> pp. 314-315 and p. 396.

11

Catholics without faith and Jews without knowledge but wishing to be Jews." The Old Testament was important to the Dutch in the practice of their own religion and they began to see Jews differently, and to accept them.[11]

As a result of this Open Door policy, Amsterdam developed into an important Jewish center, complete with significant religious institutions and leaders. To the Jews, it was 'The New Jerusalem.'"[12]

Dutch Jews became financially active in the Dutch West India Company, which was then colonizing former Spanish islands in the Caribbean. The old ignorance about Sephardim and their real religious alliances existed in Holland's colonies, and Sephardim had to struggle for early liberties there. Peter Stuyvesant, the Dutch Governor of New Amsterdam (later New York) and subsequently of Curaçao, lost his battles to have them removed.

Jews became very active not only in Holland but in its colonies as well. The Dutch decided as early as 1588 that in their relationship with the Sephardim, the government of the Netherlands would extend diplomatic and military recognition to all Jews. At a time when Jews had no European citizenship, pirates and privateers could take Jews and their property for ransom without any official protest. The Dutch, then, were the first European power to cloak Jews with this important governmental protection.[13]

The adventurous Sephardim understood the opportunities and the chance for freedom that could be forged in the New Lands. This dream impelled them to begin the first open migration of Jews to the New World. Their arrival in Dutch territories, beginning with Recife (now part of Brazil) in 1630, marked the first open westward migration of Jews. It continued through the 19th and 20th centuries, as millions came to America.

---

[11] For the tombstone inscription of Batsheva Abundiente, see this book's section of Nevis, which sets forth the 18 decipherable stones in the graveyard.

[12] Bodian, Hebrews of the Portuguese Nation, p. 58 and SCA

[13] Tolkowsky, They Took to the Sea, pp. 208-209

Spanish and Portuguese Jews were so widely known, their true religion was no longer a secret in most places to which they traveled. Among international traders, they were called the "Portuguese Nation." Indeed, in a sense they were a nation. They created and maintained an extensive network among themselves, which ran from Spain, Portugal and Europe to the Ottoman Empire and later to the Americas. They kept, through familial connections and business ties, their common Hispanic background, Marrano experience and, of course, their religion.[14]

To be known as Portuguese among Christians was synonymous with being a Jew. Family names such as Henriques, Robles, Mendes, Nuñes, Castro and Ribera were well-known as Sephardic patronyms.[15]

Sephardim referred to themselves as *'La Nación.'* It was an exclusive club. Its members, from the 1600s on, almost always founded the earliest Jewish settlements in Western Europe and the Western Hemisphere, and earned the choicest commercial and social positions within these new communities.

---

[14] Bodian, op. cit. pp 54-56

[15] Bogen, Davis S., "Mathias de Sousa: Maryland's first Colonist of African Descent", Maryland Historical Magazine, Spring 2001, p. 68. Bogen traces the arrival to Maryland of the mulatto de Sousa, who had non-African ancestors and was exposed to a European culture. Bogen advances the theory that it is likely de Sousa had a Spanish or Portuguese ancestor: "...the name is also found in Spain among Spanish and Portuguese Jews."

3

Recife: Cradle of Caribbean Jewry; Rock of Israel

Marranos had been living secretly in Portuguese Brazil as early as 1502. As New Christians, they were able to settle by Royal Grant. But within three decades, the Inquisition had been installed, driving practicing Jews underground.[1]

New Christians such as Salvador Correia were operating sugar mills and sailing ships, exporting sugar to Europe. But the Brazilian Inquisition dealt harshly with secret Jews – when it could find them.

More Jews came to Recife and freedom with the Dutch West India Trading Company in 1630, following Holland's capture of the Southwestern territory of Perambuco from Portugal. For almost a quarter century, Recife's Jews engaged in sugar and other tropical crop cultivation, finance, export and the slave trade. They built a synagogue, *Tzur Israel*, (Rock of Israel.) They opened a religious school and by 1642 brought a rabbi from Amsterdam, Isaac Aboab de Fonseca, together with a *hazzan*, Moses Rafael de Aguilar, who ministered to their congregations in the New World. They were the first rabbi and *hazzan* in the Western Hemisphere.

Isaac Aboab de Fonseca was 24 when he came to Recife, and was the community's rabbi for 13 years. Aside from being the first rabbi in the New World, he is the author of the oldest known

---

[1] Lewin, "The Crypto Jews who Colonized Brazil," Jewish Digest, 1970.

Hebrew document in the Americas.[2] Isaac Aboab de Fonseca later became Chief Rabbi of Amsterdam.[3]

Altogether, approximately 1,500 to 5,000 Sephardim settled in Recife, numbering at times one-third to one-half of the colony's European population.[4]

But the Portuguese did not surrender easily. Incited by a religious obligation to rid the conquered colony of its heretics, Jesuits spurred the Portuguese king on by reminding him that these Jews had escaped from Portugal in order to return to Judaism, and thus required punishment.[5]

Their continuing guerrilla actions harassed the Dutch. Finally, after a quarter of a century of Dutch rule, Recife once more fell to the Portuguese. January 25, 1654 was a dismal day for the Recife Jews. After 25 years of Dutch occupation, Portuguese soldiers marched into their city and following the soldiers came the Inquisition and renewed Jewish persecution.

All Jews had to find a new home. The surrendering Dutch authorities insisted upon safe passage for its Jewish subjects, to which the Portuguese agreed, granting them a time limit with which to leave.[6]

The Portuguese destroyed all evidence of Jewish presence in Recife. We do not know where the old cemeteries were. No remains of the synagogue exist. Yet persistent rumors of a synagogue once located in the heart of Recife, a city one and a half million, were confirmed. In 1999, archeologists located a *mikveh* in the basement of a downtown commercial building on one of Recife's busiest streets, once known as *Rua Do Judea* (Street of the Jews) and now called The Street of the Benevolent Jesus.[7]

---

[2] American Jewish Historical Society "The First Rabbi in the New World"

[3] Roth, History of the Marranos, p. 286

[4] Lewin, op. cit.

[5] American Jewish Historical Society

[6] Lewin, op. cit.

[7] Rohter, Larry, "A Brazilian City Resurrects its Buried Jewish Past," New York Times International Edition, May 19, 2000.

No one knows what the Western Hemisphere's first synagogue looked like, but we now know where the *mikveh* was located and its dimensions. After extensive investigation, a new synagogue rises where the old one once stood, reconstructed from plans prepared for the original synagogue.

Thus, only a relatively small band of Sephardim, who opted to remain in the Western Hemisphere instead of returning to Holland, became the nucleus of settlements which spread throughout the New World. At the time of the Recife Diaspora, the Caribbean already was divided between Holland, France, England, Denmark and Spain. Spanish islands, of course, were not open to Sephardim. French territories were a bit friendlier but whatever doors may have been open were sealed in 1685 with the enactment of the infamous *Code Noir*, which banned Jewish settlements on French islands.

Holland, England and Denmark permitted Jewish immigration. It was obvious at the start of each country's colonizing efforts that some form of economic stability had to be established on islands thousands of miles from Europe. In the days when contact between Mother Country and colony was a month or more away by perilous sea voyage, it was essential that island economies be self-sufficient. It was believed that the presence of Jews could help accomplish this end.

West Indian Jews did perform this role well, and were rewarded with civil and religious liberties and economic freedom much more quickly than Jews living in European lands. What ensued was a remarkable flowering of Caribbean Jewry. For over two centuries it dominated, influenced and shaped the force of Judaism in the New World. Members of *La Nación* became active in the 'Royal Highway,' the trading merchant's golden triangle that ran from England and Europe to the West Indies and from there to the American mainland.

Jews were traders on the sea. By establishing consortiums with other merchants, they could now own and operate their own vessels. They engaged in commercial trade with Europe. They were privateers, preying on the vessels flying enemy flags – an honorable profession at the time. And they supplied the armed forces of any country, including the young rebels of the American nation, an act which in 1781 was to be the undoing of the Jews on the Dutch island of St. Eustatius.

4

THE DUTCH CARIBBEAN

Surinam

Curaçao

St. Eustatius

Sint Maarten

Aruba

The Dutch Caribbean:
Surinam

It all started here. Surinam was the first and is still the oldest continuous Jewish community in the West Indies.[1]

It is not geographically part of the Caribbean. Surinam, or Dutch Guyana as it was formerly known, lies east of Venezuela and about 300 miles south of Barbados. While Surinam is attached to the South American mainland, its 400,000 citizens do not share that continent's history of Spanish domination, revolution and language.

Surinam has always been West Indian because of its political and trading associations with Caribbean islands. Its Dutch Associations detached it from the stormy politics of South America. In May 1993, Surinam filed for and received membership in CARICOM, the Caribbean Economic Community, and official recognition of her rightful place as a Caribbean nation.[2]

It was in Surinam where Jews first settled openly in any Caribbean community. The earliest recorded migration, in 1536, was made up of crypto-Jews fleeing the Inquisition newly installed in Brazil. In 1639, for the first time, a small group of openly professing Jews arrived in Surinam and founded a plantation

---

[1] The first permanent settlement in Surinam dates to 1639, predating Curaçao by 12 years. See Surinam Jewish Community Information Bulletin, 1991. Although the Recife Jewish settlement predates Surinam's by almost a decade, it no longer exists. It is, however, the first formal Jewish community in the New World.

[2] "Surinam to Join Caribbean Community," San Juan Star, May 26, 1993.

called Torarica, also known as Thorarica. It is said that this name was derived from the words 'Torah rica,' which in the Spanish language is 'rich Torah.' Surinam became a formal English colony founded by Lord Willoughby of Parkam, who ruled Surinam from Barbados beginning in 1650.

There had to have been some sort of formal Jewish community, since a ketubah (wedding contract) survives from the period. It was executed by rabbis and bears the date 14 Elul 5403 (1643).[3]

A second, more organized group arrived from England in 1652, under the sponsorship of Lord Willoughby. Through Willoughby's efforts, a permanent settlement was established in Surinam's interior.

The liberal Lord Willoughby ceded remarkable rights to the Jews, to encourage their settlement in this inhospitable tropical wilderness. In 1665, by fiat of the colony's General Council, Jews were permitted religious freedom, including the right to construct their own house of worship, and political autonomy, the right of self-defense and ownership of agricultural tracts along Cassipora Creek by the Surinam River. A rich agricultural community flourished, called Joden Savanne (Savannah of the Jews).[4]

The Jews organized their own militia. Early Jewish defenders led by Captain Isaac and others Pinto fought pirates, slave uprisings, Indians and French marauders from the nearby colony of French Guyana.[5]

A third and the most important wave of settlers came from Recife, led by David Nassi, also known as Joseph Nuñes de Fonseca. They became active in Joden Savanne and significantly enlarged its population and strength. By 1665, the community had erected its first synagogue, Beracha Ve Shalom (Blessings of Peace,) possibly the first synagogue in the Caribbean.[6]

---

[3] Surinam Jewish Community Bulletin, 1991

[4] Luxner, Larry, "Tropical Sanctuary," National Jewish Monthly, July/August 1994.

[5] Roth, History of the Marranos, p. 292

[6] Luxner, Larry, "Reclaiming Joden Savanne," Americas, 1995

In 1667 the British, by the treaty of Breda with the Dutch, exchanged Surinam for New Amsterdam (New York City). In the exchange of power, the new Dutch rulers reluctantly continued the liberal policies granted by the English.

Even more Jews came to Surinam in 1685, forced to leave French Guyana because of the anti-Jewish statues of the *Code Noir*. They, too, settled in the *Joden Savanne* and they established a second synagogue. It was the first time any Jewish community in the Northern Hemisphere had two synagogues.

Dutch census records indicate that over 100 Jewish families, almost 600 people with 9,000 slaves, two cemeteries, two synagogues and many plantations were counted in the *Joden Savanne* by 1694. So prosperous and flourishing was the colony that Jews from as far as Livorno, Italy, came to seek their fortunes. By 1730, more than one quarter of all plantations in the colony belonged to Jews.[7]

In 1716, the Dutch government donated land for construction of a synagogue in Paramaribo, Surinam's major city. *Neve Shalom* was completed by 1734 and Jews began leaving the *Joden Savanne* to establish themselves in the growing city.[8]

The Sephardim ceded *Neve Shalom* in 1736 to Ashkenazim (Central and Eastern European Jews) known as *Hoogduitsche*, after a bitter communal quarrel in which the Dutch government was forced to intercede and mediate. One of the conditions of the turnover was that the Ashkenazim perpetually maintain the Sephardic ritual. The Sephardim erected a second synagogue in Paramaribo, called *Tsedek Ve Shalom*, and followed the tradition of other Sephardic Caribbean synagogues by spreading sand on its floors. *Tsedek Ve Shalom*, while still standing, has shipped the entire contents of its interior to Israel for installation in Israel's Jewish Museums.[9]

---

[7] Cohen, op. cit., p. 142

[8] Ibid, p. 143

[9] Ronnen, Meir, "Israel Museum Receives 18th Century Surinam Synagogue," Jerusalem Post, Sept. 10, 1999.

Migration from the *Joden Savanne* to Paramaribo increased when, in 1832, a fire ran through the Savanna's old quarter, destroying it almost completely. The remaining Jews of the old quarter now became residents of the city.[10] At the close of the 19th Century, 1,500 Jews lived in Surinam, a considerable number for a Caribbean community.

Surinam's Jews have always maintained contact with other Jews of the Western Hemisphere. Kosher meat was imported from New York, among other places, beginning in the 1760s. The Surinam congregation received pleas from Philadelphia's *Mikve Israel* synagogue for building donations in 1782. And there were building requests from Newport, Rhode Island and Lancaster, Pennsylvania. Rabbis and *hazzanim* (cantors) left Paramaribo to lead congregations on the American mainland.

In 1792, David de Isaac Cohen Nassy, a physician and direct descendant of the founder of Surinam's Jewish community, immigrated to Philadelphia. He was that city's first Jewish doctor. Almost immediately after his arrival, the city was struck with a yellow fever epidemic. At that time, medicine's knowledge of the disease was limited. Nassy successfully treated 98 of the 117 patients seen by him. Working with other West Indian and French-trained doctors, he was able to use cool baths, fluids and other treatments to relieve the epidemic.

Today, Surinam's few remaining Jews live in Paramaribo. They are remnants of a declining community, lost to assimilation and migrations to Holland and the United States. They are not generally of the merchant class. Many are high-level civil servants. Because of the limited number of congregants, religious services alternated between Ashkenazic *Neve Shalom* (still adhering to Sephardic ritual according to the 1736 agreement) and Sephardic *Tzedek Ve Shalom* synagogues (before its closing), the two communities having long settled their communal differences. A significant number of Surinam's Jews are of African descent, the offspring of ethnically mixed unions. Many practicing Jews are

---

[10] Surinam Jewish Community Bulletin, 1999

former Christians who have converted without a rabbi's instruction.[11]

Surinam's Jews seem to be well integrated within their community. Next to *Neve Shalom*, a Muslim mosque thrives, without any conflict between the two religions.[12]

In 1968 and again in 1992, the government of Surinam commemorated Jewish presence in its country. A series of three stamps were issued in 1968. One depicts a map of the *Joden Savanne* and the names of plantation owners Nassy, DeCasseres, Nuñes de Costa, De Silva and De Pinto. *Joden Savanne's* plantations bore biblical names such as Hebron and Carmel, which are also memorialized.

A second stamp shows a sailing ship passing below *Beracha V'Shalom* Synagogue, which rises upon the heights of a hill. The third stamp depicts a typical Caribbean Sephardic gravestone with its unique carvings and markings (see stamp illustrations).

Another stamp issued in 1992 commemorates Sephardim and their contribution to Surinam's development. It features a sailing ship with the word 'Sepharad', a *menorah*, and the Star of David.

Stamp depicting the map of the *Joden Savanne* with the names of Jewish plantation owners.

---

[11] Luxner, Larry, "Tropical Sanctuary" July/August 1994.

[12] French, Howard W. "In a Surinam Jumble; the Quest for Identity," New York Times International Edition. October 23, 1990. Also Luxner's "Reclaiming Joden Savanne."

Stamp depicting a typical gravestone in Surinam

Paramaribo's community is still aware of its importance in New World Jewish history and their contributions to Surinam. It held ceremonies in 1992 at *Joden Savanne*, designed to remember and explain the Jewish experience in the *Joden Savanne* and Surinam.

Today, the *Joden Savanne* lies abandoned beneath a tangle of thick underbrush within the jungles of Surinam. The crumbling foundations of *Beracha V'Shalom* can still be seen, as can gravestones and other monuments of the old Jewish cemetery.

Access to the old community is becoming increasingly difficult because of deteriorating roads and guerrilla activity in the jungle.[13] The community has requested funds for maintenance, but troubled with its own economic woes, Surinam is unable to advance the funds.

In a wry twist, interned Nazi sympathizers during World War II were sent to a camp in *Joden Savanne* and put to work in the old Savanna, restoring Jewish cemeteries and structures. The result of their work was, in time, lost once again because of the jungle's growth.[14]

---

[13] Letter from René Fernandez, President, Surinam Sephardic Community, 1992. Also Brooks, A.A., "A Jungle Journey." Also Farah, Douglas, "The Ruins of Jewish Savannah," <u>Washington Post,</u> October 31, 1997.

[14] "In a Surinam Jumble;" "Reclaiming Joden Savanne;" "Tropical Sanctuary;" "A Jungle Journey." Also Farah Douglass, "The Ruins of Jewish Savannah," <u>Washington Post</u>, October 31, 1997.

Middle-aged Surinam Jews can still remember when as children they took trips to the *Joden Savanne* to visit the old cemeteries and the synagogue. Today, this is impossible because of the undergrowth, the presence of guerillas, and squatters. As a result, the *Joden Savanne* goes completely untended, resulting in irreparable deterioration of its remaining structures and gravestones.

By the end of the 19th Century, 150 Jews lived in Surinam, both Sephardic and Ashkenazic. They have not had a permanent rabbi since 1969. The World Population Review, however, estimates the number of Jews on the island in 2020, to be 200.

Stamp depicting the Synagogue built in 1685

The Dutch Caribbean: Curaçao

If ever a safety valve existed for Jews in the New World, it was Curaçao. Two decades after Holland conquered Curaçao, the Dutch West India Company invited Jews to settle on this 448 square-kilometer island just off the coast of Venezuela. Although some did arrive in 1651, they soon left because the land could not support agriculture.[1]

A small group of 70 refugees from Recife, led by Isaac da Costa, arrived in 1659. This second attempt at Jewish colonization focused upon commerce, which was the touchstone to the outstanding success of the Jewish community of Curaçao and the beginning of Judaism's most important presence the West Indies.[2]

For almost 200 years, Curaçao was to be the home of the premier congregation of the Western Hemisphere. It provided money, religious assistance and other needs to new Jewish communities forming throughout the Americas. It set the tone for Jewish life in much of North America and parts of the South American mainland.

For over 150 years, Curaçao had the largest Jewish population in the New World.[3] *Mikve Israel-Emanuel* is still the oldest synagogue in continuous use in the Western Hemisphere, and the congregation celebrated its 350th anniversary in April 2001.

---

[1] "Our 'Snoa,' 5492-5742, Cong. Mikve-Israel," p. 12, Joao d'Yilan or Juan Ilian, envisioned an agricultural community. Because of lack of ground water and arable soil, this venture failed.

[2] Cohen, op. cit p. 147.

[3] "Our 'Snoa', 5992-5742," p. 42-44

In building their synagogue, Curaçao's Jews adopted the architectural arrangement of the Spanish and Portuguese Synagogue of Amsterdam, their mother synagogue. This meant that Curaçao's synagogue was physically constructed with the *bimah* (reader's platform) in the center facing the Ark at the Eastern wall. Congregants faced each other from benches (*bancas*) on both sides of the room, the *bemah* and the Ark in the middle.[4]

Women were separated from men in the traditional Orthodox manner, in an upper gallery reached from an outside stairway. Upper galleries in the Caribbean are unique by being accessed through outside stairways, since the climate was not inhospitable.

Sand covers the floor. There are several explanations regarding this practice. Some commentators say the sand is to remind congregants of the silence in which their ancestors were forced to pray, to escape the inquisitors' deadly detection. Others say that the sand symbolized the desert across which Moses led the children of Israel for 40 years.[5]

Interesting Aside:

All synagogues of Sephardic origin in the colonial Caribbean had or have sand on their floors. These include synagogues in current use in Jamaica, St. Thomas, Curaçao and Surinam. According to Paul Altman of Barbados, the Barbados synagogue originally had sand covering its black and white marble checkerboard floors. When it was rebuilt in 1832 after a hurricane had damaged the building, sand was not replaced. Thus, what today's congregant sees is the original floor existing after 1832.

The existing synagogues of Havana, Cuba, all of the 20th century, one of which is Sephardic, have no sand. The three synagogues of Puerto Rico, all of which have Ashkenazic roots, have no sand, nor do the synagogues in

---

[4] Ibid., p. 30

[5] Synagogue Guidebook, Cong. Mikve Israel-Emanuel, Curaçao 1964. See also A Short History of the Hebrew Congregation of St. Thomas (including a forward by former St. Thomas resident and novelist, Herman Wouk.) 1983 (un-paginated).

Aruba and the Dominican Republic, all of recent origin. The synagogue of Martinique, erected in 1997, is North African Sephardic, not following Spanish and Portuguese rituals and history, and has no sand on its floors.

While the rabbi of the period, Simon J. Maslin, states the sand represents the desert through which Moses led the children of Israel, he suggests another reason: to keep the sanctuary quiet. Other sources I set out here give other reasons: the sand represents the numerous children of Israel, "You shall be as numerous as the sands of the sea," (Genesis: 22:17) or that the sand deadened the footfalls of the congregants to keep them from the prying Inquisition. Rabbi Emmanuel states that aside from emulating the tabernacle of the Israelites in the desert, Portuguese Jews used sand to muffle their footsteps. This included a mixture of sand imported from Jerusalem.[6] I personally subscribe to the latter interpretation.

The reader should note that all synagogues in the colonial West Indies and colonial America, including Montreal (and Bevis Marks synagogue of London) follow the first great synagogue constructed in Western Europe in Amsterdam, in 1675 by *Marranos* escaping from Spain and Portugal. The West Indies is the only other place, besides Amsterdam however, where sand is spread over sanctuary floors.

Spanish, Portuguese and Hebrew were used in the synagogue service until the middle of the 19th Century. The same strict congregational rules and regulations (*hascamoth*) that were then in force in Amsterdam – resulting in the excommunication of philosophers/thinkers Benedict Spinoza and Uriel D'Acosta – were put into use on this Caribbean Island. These rules had to be approved by Prince William II of Holland in 1751. Later amendments were approved by Princess Anne in 1755.[7]

---

[6] Emmanuel, op. cit., p. 231.

[7] Ibid, p. 231

The reader should not be surprised that the Dutch government became involved with synagogue procedure and deportment. Throughout the history of this enlightened country, Dutch officials have resolved disputes between Sephardim and Ashkenazim in Surinam and Curaçao and elsewhere. Here are only a few examples: They gave Sephardim a tract of land in Paramaribo, Surinam's main city, to build a second synagogue, ending a community dispute between Sephardim and Ashkenazim.[8]

In 1865 the colonial government of Curaçao donated to the Dutch Jewish Reform Synagogue (Temple Emanuel) a plot of land 40 by 50 meters to construct their place of Worship.[9]

The result was that from very early on, synagogues in the West Indies and American mainland adopted the Curaçao architecture and, to an extent, the Amsterdam rules. Even synagogues built in English colonies followed this design. London's Spanish and Portuguese Bevis Marks Synagogue, which is England's first synagogue, owes its design and creation to the Mother Synagogue of Amsterdam. Curiously, the only two Sephardic synagogues that depart from this design by not having an upper gallery, is that of St. Thomas, which was a Danish colony, and Barbados, which originally had sand. After Barbados' building was restored, no sand was put on the floor. Otherwise, the St. Thomas and Barbados synagogues follow the Sephardic placement of bimah, Ark and benches.

Interesting Aside:

Technically speaking, while the St. Thomas synagogue does not have an upper gallery, its arrangement on one floor includes a section just one step higher than the rest of the seating. It was here, when St. Thomas followed the Orthodox Sephardic rituals that women sat apart from men. In a section of the newsletter

---

[8] Surinam Jewish Community Bulletin, 1991.

[9] Emmanuel, op. cit. p. 387. See also p. 207 where the Chief of Police of Willemstadt, Curaçao, interceded in a community quarrel; colonial officials also kept peace among Sephardim and Ashkenazim in St. Eustatius.

> for the St. Thomas Congregation, March 1993, David
> Stanley Sasso, who billed himself as "the second eldest
> male Sephardic Jew on St. Thomas," wrote an article
> called "St. Thomas of Yesteryear." In the article, Sasso
> recalls that as a youth, "Jews and Jewesses were
> forbidden to sit together... men sat on the lower
> benches, while women sat on the above benches." This
> occurred before the Congregation adopted Reform
> Judaism.

So influential was Curaçao that a religious writer in 1746 called Curaçao "Queen Mother of all the islands in America."[10]

Curaçao's rabbis made circuits throughout the Caribbean, ministering to congregations lacking spiritual leaders. Curaçao was the place to which both Caribbean and mainland Jews looked for religious guidance. This island community not only provided a religious example for all American Jewry, but they often assisted with financial aid and gave religious artifacts to new congregations and synagogues. This was true not only for the West Indies, but on the North American mainland as well. Synagogues in New York, Philadelphia, Newport and Savannah were among the beneficiaries.[11]

In 1730, the Curaçao Jewish community sent $379 worth of copper to New York's Spanish and Portuguese congregation, *Shearith Israel*, to help construct its Mill Street Synagogue, the first in colonial America. A letter accompanying the gift read, *"Yevarech Hakahal Beshalom Bevo E Veyiskon Bekhavod Bi-Shearith Israel."* (May the Lord in His coming bless the congregation with peace and May He dwell with Honor in *Shearith Israel*.)"[12]

---

[10] Emmanuel, op. cit., p.180. The statement was made by David Aboab, a visiting Talmudic student from Holland.

[11] Ibid, p. 165.

[12] Grinstein, The Rise of the Jewish Community of New York 1654-1860, p. 407.

Curacao's Temple *Emmanuel*, built in 1864.
The congregation merged with *Mikve Israel* in 1964.

By the mid-1700s, at the eve of the American Revolution, the island's approximately 2,000 Jews were 50 percent of its European population, a significantly greater number than all Jews on the North American mainland.[13] When one considers that in 1800, Charlestown, South Carolina, the largest Jewish community in the United States, was home to 500 Jews, and that there were only

---

[13] Karner, op. cit., p. 29.

2,500 Jews in the entire American Republic, Curaçao and the rest of the Caribbean loom large as influential communities in the Western Hemisphere. The 1745 census in Curaçao listed 1,400 Jews; by 1750, it was 2,000. In 1785, there were 1,200 and by 1789, there were 1,495. The reason for the fluctuation is simple. As business opportunities arose, male Sephardim formed colonies in Maracaibo and Coro in Venezuela, St. Thomas, Aruba, Jamaica, Santo Domingo and Central America. With Hispanic family names and fluency in Spanish, Curaçao's young men easily fit into Latin societies.[14]

Unlike Barbados, Jamaica, St. Thomas and Nevis, Curaçao's soil was not fertile, so the community engaged in other commercial enterprises such as shipping, insurance, and banking. The Maduro family was heavily engaged in many of these enterprises including the Maduro Bank. Jews became so important in island society that one 20th Century rabbi has remarked that outside of Israel, he knew of no other place where Jews were so represented as in "the 400 of Curaçao."[15] Curaçao's Jews, especially its Sephardim, retain a strong pride in their Judaism and ancestral roots, which most trace to Iberia.

The gate leading to the oldest Jewish cemetery in continuous use in the Western Hemisphere. Note the refinery in the background. Its fumes damaged many stones.

Curaçao's Sephardim supported Simon Bolivar during the South American Revolution, as did most of

---

[14] Karner, op. cit., pp. 26-38.

[15] Maslin, Rabbi Simon. "Curaçao." National Jewish Monthly, September 1964.

Curaçao. Called "The Liberator of South America," Bolivar sought and received refuge at the home of Abraham de Meza after his defeat at Puerto Cabello.

The first of Bolivar's champions from Curaçao was Mordechy Ricardo, an attorney. Several members of Curaçao's Jews fought with Bolivar and participated in the battles that wrenched Venezuela and Colombia from Spain. Bolivar received money and credit for arms purchases from the island's Sephardic merchants who assisted in financing his revolution.[16]

Curaçao offers much material for the seekers of Jewish history. *Mikve Israel-Emanuel* is the oldest synagogue building in continuous use in the Americas. It dates to 1731. Congregation *Emanuel's* synagogue was built in 1864. Emanuel merged with *Mikve Israel* in 1965. Its tall, distinct steeple still stands, a short walk from *Mikve Israel-Emanuel.*

A 300-year old *mikve* (ritual bath) was unearthed during street restorations in the 1970s and can still be seen today. There is a Jewish museum near the synagogue. Streets and monuments throughout the island are named for prominent Curaçao families, such as Maduro, Capriles and Salas. Curaçao's Jews have been doctors, members of the island's militia, lawyers, important businessmen and movers of the island's economy.

Perhaps the most dramatic testimony to the close partnership between Curaçao and its Jews are its cemeteries. They are some of the oldest Jewish burial grounds in the Western Hemisphere still in use, dating from 1659.[17] Because of their location next to an oil refinery in the 1960s and 1970s, the fumes were causing the tombstones to deteriorate. They were painted with chemicals to prevent decay.

Some 2,000 decipherable stones are located at the island's old cemetery. Names of Jews whose descendants are still active in

---

[16]Emmanuel, op. cit., pp. 295-301.

[17] Emmanuel, Precious Stones of the Jews of Curaçao, page 34; also Cohen op. cit., and article titled "Stones of Memory: Revelation from a Cemetery in Curaçao," p. 81-140 by Rochelle Weinstein.

Curaçao society can be found inscribed on elaborate stones, many hundreds of years old. These are not the sorts of stones you will find in other Jewish graveyards. They are carved in Hebrew, Spanish, Portuguese and Dutch. What makes them special are the unique and elaborate scenes depicting the professions of the deceased, such as sailing ships and physician's implements.[18] Also carved on the stones are non-Jewish symbols, such as the Grim Reaper's scythe, hourglass and skull and crossbones. There are carved details of the dying during their last moments on their deathbeds.

Because there were no marble or limestone quarries in the Caribbean, families had to send to Italy for the stones and then ship them to Holland for carving. Sometimes the sculptors were not Jewish and were not always familiar with the requirements of Jewish law or its symbols. As a result, rabbis are sometimes depicted without skullcaps, errors are made in Hebrew dates and spelling, and non-Jewish symbols are plentiful.[19]

Curaçao gravestones are not only rich with the history, professions and depictions of social class, but they are a record of the other places from which Jews were attracted to this island. Throughout the Caribbean, old Sephardic cemeteries have the same look, if not the size, of the Curaçao cemetery.[20]

Besides the Sephardim, Curaçao is home to an active Ashkenazic community of approximately 175. They maintain their own synagogue, *Shaare Tzedek*, and hold regular services. Ashkenazim have been active in Curaçao's life for almost a century.

There are about 350 Jews living in Curaçao. They maintain two active synagogues but are unable to maintain a rabbi. Nonetheless, a Chabad community was organized in Curaçao early in the 21st

---

[18] Emmanuel, I. and S., A History of the Jews of the Netherlands Antilles. The Emmanuels documented 225 Jewish ship's captains from 1698 to 1881. There are over 1,000 Jewish ship owners for the corresponding period.

[19] Ibid, p. 74; also Emmanuel, Precious Stones of the Jews of Curaçao, p. 123-129.

[20] Ibid. Emmanuel devotes almost all of this book to the epitaphs and photographs of the famous *Bet Haim* (graveyard) at Blenheim.

Century. Their leader is Rabbi Rafael Silver. The Sephardic community has been steadily dwindling.[21]

In April 2001, at the 350th Anniversary ceremonies of the founding of one of the oldest Jewish community in the Western Hemisphere, the chairman of the festivities, Ron Gomes Casseres, stated that Sephardic life on the island has "become improbable."[22]

Despite this, Jews will continue to live in Curaçao and earn their livelihoods here. What will cease, as has occurred on all Caribbean islands, is the continuity of the Spanish and Portuguese families who once dominated the region with their unique culture. *La Nación* no longer has meaning in terms of economic and social power. It is an historic memory, a binding influence only for those few families who have survived the centuries of integration in the modern world.

---

[21] Letter from I. Grynzstein, Cong. *Shaare Tzedek* (The Ashkenazic congregation of Curaçao), Curaçao, 1992. The community was founded in 1926, augmenting Ashkenazim that preceded them. By 1959, they had put together two buildings to erect their synagogue. Emmanuel, op. cit., p. 497. Also Perry Dan, "Congregations Shrinks at Historic Synagogue," Associated Press, May 2, 1999.

[22] Rolnick, Josh, "Jewish Paradise in the Caribbean?" Moment, Washington, D.C. August 2001.

The Dutch Caribbean:
St. Eustatius

Ruines Jewish Temple and part of the Town

Honen Dalim synagogue, St. Eustatius, as it appeared on a
Dutch postcard circa 1920. Compare the building in this photo
with the photo taken in 1993, later in this chapter.[1]

It was only natural that Sephardim should settle in Holland's
New World colonies, as the Dutch were benevolent in their
treatment of Jews.

Four families first settled on the Dutch colony of St. Eustatius
(known as Statia) in 1722, although settlers from Curaçao sailed
back and forth between the islands as early as 1660. Two of the

---

[1] Photo from the collection of Gérard Silvain, as it appears in his book, *Sepharades et
Juifs d'alleurs*.

original settlers in St. Eustatius were the Cohen Henriquez and the Nuñes Neto families.[2]

Later permanent colonists requested that the Amsterdam synagogue act as their representative in the Netherlands, to seek equal religious rights for them. During the colonial period, the Spanish and Portuguese synagogues of Amsterdam and London acted as representatives to their respective governments for Jewish colonists: Statians obtained rights to build synagogues and establish cemeteries. They requested exemption from military guard duty on the Sabbath in 1730. In 1739, they received permission to erect their own synagogue, *Honen Dalim* (Merciful to the Poor).[3]

> **Interesting Aside:**
>
> Jews living on Dutch islands petitioned the authorities through the Spanish and Portuguese synagogue of Amsterdam, which in turn went through the Dutch West India Company. The Danish Virgin Islands operated through the Great Synagogue at Copenhagen. English colonists ˋpetitioned Bevis Marks synagogue in London. These three synagogues, all of Spanish and Portuguese origins, maintain the records of West Indian synagogues to this day. When communities were established during the early settlement periods, European mother synagogues often gave *Torahs* and other ritual items to new congregations. This tradition continued even to the 20th Century. When the Barbados synagogue was sold in 1929, it was London's Bevis Marks Synagogue that arranged for the sale and for the return to England of the holy scrolls and other artifacts. Bevis Marks also arranged for the perpetuation of the Barbados cemeteries.
>
> These arrangements even extend to the United States. New York's *Shearith Israel*, the Spanish and Portuguese synagogue, and America's first Jewish congregation, maintains title to the Touro Synagogue in Newport, Rhode Island, this country's oldest synagogue structure.

---

[2] Emmanuel, op. cit., p. 518.

[3] Ibid, p. 519.

Even courts recognize this relationship. When Ashkenazic worshippers wished to use the old Touro Synagogue in the late 1800s, *Shearith Israel* acceded, as long as they used the Sephardic *hazzan*. Years later the worshippers challenged the procedure and sued in court to wrest control from *Shearith Israel*. The court upheld *Shearith Israel*, which is why services are still held in the Sephardic ritual.[4]

**The ruins of Synagogue *Honen Dalim*.
The chairs and lectern were provided by the island government during a commemoration ceremony in 1993.**

[4] Cohen, op. cit., p. 162.

After a hurricane damaged the synagogue in 1772, it was rebuilt. The communities in Curaçao, Amsterdam and New York contributed money and ritual objects towards the reconstruction.[5] *Honen Dalim* may be the second oldest synagogue structure in the Western Hemisphere still partially standing. The congregation was affluent enough to have enjoyed the services of two rabbis between 1775 and 1790: Rabbi Ezekiel and Rabbi Jacob Robles.

On the eve of the American Revolution, this tiny dot in the Caribbean located between St. Thomas and St. Kitts, measuring seven square miles, was home to a thriving commercial community in which Sephardim played a leading role.

Non-agricultural St. Eustatius was an important go-between for war supplies traded between Europe and the rebel American colonies during the Revolutionary War. Sailing in neutral Dutch ships or American cutters swift enough to breach the British blockades, supplies often reached the American mainland, to the anger of the British.

St. Eustatius was a neutral free port. Trade that was illegal between other islands – at that time it was illegal for an island to trade with any other island or country not of the mother country – could pass through St. Eustatius. Cargo in neutral ships came into St. Eustatius and, after much manipulation of documents and Bills of Lading and after complicated trans-shipment of illegal cargo, could leave for the American colonies either in neutral ships or through properly documented vessels.[6]

In 1776, the American Jewish patriot Jonas Phillips sent a letter to his mother in Holland via St. Eustatius, as many other letter writers did to ensure swiftness and safe delivery. The letter contained a copy of the newly published Declaration of Independence. Phillips, writing in Yiddish to avoid British snoops, explained that a fortune could be made running the British blockade now that war had started. Unfortunately, the letter was

---

[5]Ezratty, H., *"Konmemorasion en Stratia,"* Aki Yerushalayim, Kol Israel, Jerusalem, #48, 1993. (written in Ladino).

[6] Tuchman, Barbara: The First Salute p. 19.

captured along with its Yankee sailing ship. That letter now rests in the British Publication office, with a 200 year old scholar's note saying that the unintelligible Yiddish must be some sort of shorthand.

The remains of what is believed to be a ritual *mikvah*. The interior contains a piping system to bring fresh water from an extinct volcano crater. The site is now used for voodoo rites and often contains bones of sacrificed goats.

That same year, the American trading ship *Andria Doria* entered St. Eustatius' Oranjestad harbor, her mast flying the colors of the new rebel Republic. Dutch Governor De Graff enthusiastically ordered an 11-gun salute fired from Fort Orange located high above the waterfront.[7]

Admiral Rodney, commander of England's Caribbean squadron, was furious when he learned of this event. He knew that the Dutch island, also known as the Golden Rock, or Statia, was trading with the rebels. Rodney was also aware that much of the shipping and trading on Statia was in Jewish hands. But there was little he could do about it.[8]

Statia was Dutch territory and England was not then at war with Holland. British ships had to be satisfied with trying to stop rebel and other enemy ships laden with military supplies after they left the island and sailed into international waters. Often, the Yankees were too fast for the British and would out-run them to safety.

But Rodney would eventually have his revenge. When he did, he acted swiftly and ruthlessly. In his view, St. Eustatius was home to a nest of vipers and he was determined to eliminate the fangs directed at his heart.

On February 3, 1781, after Holland and England had declared war on one another, Rodney sailed into Oranjestad harbor. Without firing a shot (the Dutch on St. Eustatius were unaware that war had been declared), he captured its warehouses and emptied them of their contents. Rodney loaded his ships with booty, some $15 million worth. He also captured 130 merchant ships then at anchor in the Harbor and appropriated their wares. He then ordered his sailors to pursue 30 more ships that had just set sail for Europe.[9]

In all, Rodney captured 160 ships and sent the plunder back to England. He might have become a rich man with his share of the

---

[7] "Statia's Historic Salute," <u>Bulletin of the Government of St. Eustatius.</u>

[8] Ezratty, op. cit.

[9] Tuchman, op. cit. p. 97.

loot, but the convoy was seized by French vessels, allies of the Dutch. Rodney saw none of his booty; it was returned to Statia.

The island's capture was a great loss to the Americans. There had been almost 2,000 sailors in the Harbor that February day, most willing to fight. But they were captured, as the British had the foresight to cut off their supplies.[10]

A Jewish gravestone inscribed in Portuguese, in St. Eustatius.

---

[10] Ibid. p. 96.

Then Rodney committed a controversial act: He arrested all of Statia's merchants and banished them to the British islands of St. Kitts and Antigua. Many of the merchants were Jews. They represented a substantial part of the exiled Statians.

Strictly speaking, it was not an anti-Semitic act but one aimed at tradesmen who had supplied Rodney's enemies. But Jews were singled out for special treatment: They were given only one day's notice to leave; they were strip-searched; they were robbed of their personal possessions. Rodney's soldiers were ordered to rip the linings of their clothing in search of money and other valuables.

Perhaps Rodney remembered the role Jewish merchants played in assisting the American rebels. In addition to these indignities, he extorted £8,000 from Jewish merchants. One old man, Samuel Hoheb, was relieved of gold coins found sewn into the lining of his coat. Another Jew, Jacob Pollack, who had been expelled from the American colonies for his pro-British leanings, was also robbed of his cash. The English considered him an enemy merely because he was a Jewish merchant on St. Eustatius.[11]

The banishment disrupted the entire Jewish community. When London learned of Rodney's actions, a furor arose. But the general consensus in Parliament, which debated the event, was that the Admiral was not racially motivated. Rodney, trying to justify his acts, subsequently wrote of St. Eustatius, "Instead of the greatest emporium on earth ... [it is] a mere desert and only known by report."[12]

So devastating was his attack that it was prominently mentioned in an equal rights petition of the Jews of Philadelphia made in 1791 to the American government, to underscore the suffering Jews had endured in order to help the new American Republic.[13]

Although the banished merchants returned to St. Eustatius shortly thereafter (perhaps as a result of petitions protesting the

---

[11] Emmanuel, op. cit., p. 523-526.

[12] Tuchman, op. cit. p. 103.

[13] Schappes, M.U. , Documentary History of the Jews of the U.S. 1654-1875, p. 63.

injustice from Englishmen on the islands to which they had been sent) the community never entirely recovered. Rodney had put the island to the torch after he stripped it bare. Within 20 years, most Jews left, many for the Danish island of St. Thomas, where they founded the community that was to become home to the oldest continuously used synagogue building under the United States flag.

Descendants of Philip Waag, once one of the wealthiest Jews on St. Eustatius, continued in residence until 1843. By 1850, here were only three Jews left on St. Eustatius.[14]

Until recently, the walls of the old synagogue, *Honen Dalim*, still remained, although the roof and the second floor are long gone. The outside stairway to its second story gallery leads nowhere, as the second floor has been stripped for its building materials. Goats frequented the ruins, so wire mesh has been installed to keep them out.

The street on which *Honen Dalim* is located is still known as Jew's Way. A small cemetery, about half a mile away, contains the graves of Sephardim who lived here more than two centuries ago. The stone wall surrounding the cemetery has two iron gates. One bears a representation of the Ten Commandments; the other, the date 1739, the year of the cemetery's consecration.

In 1981, the forgotten Jewish place came back to life, if only briefly. A group of Boy Scouts from New Jersey cleared away the underbrush inside the ruined walls so that one of them could celebrate his Bar Mitzvah on this historic spot. The *Torah* used in the service was lent to them by the Sint Maarten Jewish community.[15]

Honen Dalim synagogue was used again in 1993, when a contingent of 50 Caribbean Jews from Barbados, Puerto Rico, St.

---

[14] Emmanuel, op. cit., p. 521.

[15] Letter to the author from Jane and Ed Berkowitz. The Berkowitz' retired during the winters to Sint Maarten and then Puerto Rico. It was during their years in Sint Maarten that they were instrumental in lending a Torah for use by a Bar Mitzvah group in St. Eustatius.

Croix and St. Thomas paid homage to this out-of-the-way community. They prayed there and walked among the old gravestones, under the sponsorship of the island's government.

Interesting Aside:

The colonial government not only provided our group with chairs, a podium, and a sound system, but they also fed us with an outdoor buffet in a shaded, tree-lined square. Later, we were treated to the presence of government officials who addressed us. We were told that the government was aware of the contributions Jews had made to the island in its early history and hoped that Jews would return to establish themselves once again. The address was essentially the same one I had heard over 20 years earlier at the re-consecration of the cemetery at Charlestown, Nevis. The islands are aware that for many of them, their greatest period of prosperity and economic security coincided with the presence of a Jewish community.

The island's library has a model of the synagogue as it looked over 200 years ago. Hoping to restore the structure, townspeople collect funds from tourists in an ambitious attempt to put its walls, roof and floors back together again. Considering the tiny population of this island, which is not in the mainstream of tourist traffic, it is remarkable that the government takes great care in preserving these remembrances of the Jewish people. Such solicitude needs to be duplicated elsewhere throughout the islands, where we are slowly loosing this heritage to the jungle, pollution and environmental wear and tear.

Aaron Koschitsky, a recent traveler to St. Eustatius, reports that all these efforts are proving fruitful. Restoration has begun: a new roof graces the old synagogue and the window openings have been repaired. A restored building should be available for tourists soon.

We saw the restoration described by Mr. Koschitsky in 2006. It is remarkable when one considers that this tiny island and its small population were able to muster resources to restore the old synagogue. Every Statian is involved but much of the credit goes to Gay McAllister, a non-Jewish, non-native of Statia, who is the energetic force in the restoration. She is St. Eustatius' resident historian. I have known her for years and am impressed with how she glows when speaking of Honen *Dalim*. On occasion, she cries tears of joy when speaking of the synagogue.

Interesting Aside:

In conversations with Gay McAllister,. I was impressed with the respect residents of this island give to the synagogue and cemetery. Their library, a wonderful facility considering it serves less than 2,000 people, has a scale model of *Honen Dalim* looking as it must have in its heyday. Next to the model is a box requesting donations for restoration of this symbol of the Jewish people's quest for the right to pray and live in peace. As the members of our group passed by, we all dropped coins and bills into the box. When I compared photographs I took of the old synagogue walls in 1993 with those of a decade or two earlier, it is easy to see that despite the care taken of *Honen Dalim*, there was a degree of deterioration exacting its toll on this monument. The current re-construction of the synagogue walls are a tribute to this tiny community.

Eighteen-hundred people lived on St. Eustatius in 1993. A Massachusetts couple, who have a winter retirement home there, and one permanent resident, a fisherman, were the only Jews on the island then.

Remains of the destroyed piers where Jewish
merchants maintained warehouses.

The Dutch Caribbean:
Sint Maarten

This Windward Island, 37 miles square and approximately 100 miles southeast of St. Thomas, is the world's smallest island mass divided between two countries. France and Holland share ownership of this tiny island.

Sint Maartin, as the Dutch side is known, seems to have been first settled by victims of Admiral Rodney's raid on St. Eustatius in 1781. But the refugee community never thrived. Within 40 years, the brick synagogue erected on *Acherstraat* was a pile of overgrown rubble with few, if any, Jews left on the island to worship there. It is said that the old West Indian Tavern in Phillipsburg (since razed) occupied the site of the old synagogue and that a portion of the Tavern's walls were those of the old synagogue.[1]

At the other end of Front Street, archeologists have found the remains of what is believed to be the old Jewish cemetery. Much work needs to be done for verification. There is a small street called Jew's Cemetery Lane, which seems to be part of a complex of synagogue, walkway and cemetery.[2] Such a layout is standard for many Caribbean communities.

---

[1] Hartog, Dr. J., <u>History of Sint Maarten and St. Martin</u>. Jacycees Sint Maarten, Philipsburg (no date), p. 118.

[2] <u>Bulletin of the St. Martin National Heritage Foundation</u> titled "Synagogue," contains floor plans of the synagogue and possible *mikve* with a detailed description of the remaining walls and its location. This synagogue, walkway and cemetery arrangement is similar to the one in Georgetown, Nevis. Also, see chapter on Nevis in this book.

In 1969, less than ten adult Jewish males lived permanently in Sint Maarten. But by 1971, the wave of tourism throughout the Caribbean brought a modest resurgence of permanent Jewish families and regularly returning winter tourists to the island. Settlers came from the United States, Curaçao, Surinam, the Dominican Republic, Guadeloupe and Israel. There was even a Holocaust survivor among them.

A *Rosh Hashanah* (High Holiday) service held in 1971 must have been unique: it was conducted with elements of both Ashkenazic and Sephardic ritual in an Orthodox-Conservative setting. There was no *Torah*, but a tiny souvenir scroll, plucked from a congregant's gift shop, was used as a symbol of the Book of Laws. A tourist who had purchased a *shofar* (ram's horn used for blowing notes during the New Year service) in Israel and was returning to New York with it, produced it for use during the service, blowing it with much gusto.

There was no uniform prayer book. Congregants used their own books. Each had the Hebrew text, but the second language of these books varied from English and Hungarian to Spanish, Dutch and Portuguese, the last three languages being the ones most often used by Dutch Caribbean Sephardim.[3]

Gradually, the community's efforts became known. As many as 50 to 60 permanent residents and tourists prayed together on subsequent High Holidays. The congregation even acquired its own *Torah*. Services were not offered on a regular basis, however.

About 20 Jewish families live permanently in Sint Maarten in an organized community.[4] The *Torah* reposes in a vault, under lock and key. It is the *Torah* lent to the Boy Scouts who celebrated a Bar Mitzvah on St. Eustatius in 1993 (see chapter on St. Eustatius).

---

[3] Letter from Jane and Ed Berkowitz to the author dated 1994.

[4] Conversations February 2001 with Ms. Shaw, a member of the Sint Maarten Jewish community.

The Dutch Caribbean:
Aruba

A former colony of Holland, Aruba is 20 miles long by six miles wide and a mere 25 miles off the coast of Venezuela. Aruba has not held great historical prominence in Jewish Caribbean history. At present, however, there is a small but active Jewish community among the island's 70,000 inhabitants.[1]

Although it was first settled formally in 1754 by Moses de Salomon Levy Maduro, a member of the well-known Curaçao family, and his wife and children, there is some evidence that the island hosted Jews as early as 1563. Whoever these earlier settlers may have been, they made no great impact on the island or its history.[2]

As with the Levy Maduros, others from Curaçao settled here sporadically. The lack of drinking water made living on the island difficult: most people traveled back and forth on business trips between the two Dutch islands, which are only 50 miles apart.[3]

A brief and minor flurry of Jewish migration occurred during the middle of the 19th Century, when a short-lived gold find was

[1] Berkey, Barry and Velma, "The Jewish Presence in Aruba," Washington Jewish Week; also Dec. 17, 1998, letter from Martha E. Lichtenstein, community secretary, to author.

[2] Emmanuel, op. cit., p. 529. Also Postal, op. cit., p. 11

[3] History of the First Jewish Settlers in Aruba, a bulletin provided by Beth Israel of Aruba, updated and un-paginated, circa 1993.

made at Balashi, and again when phosphate mining was introduced to the island.[4]

By 1962, the community was strong enough to erect its own synagogue, a handsome, modern, triangular structure called *Beth Israel*, located on A. Lacle Boulevard.[5]

Aruban Jews number some 120. Their size has decreased since the early 2000s. They are actively in contact with other Jewish communities and organizations in Venezuela, Israel and elsewhere; they had the services of an English rabbi who has been replaced by a cantor or *hazzan*.[6] In 2013, a Chabad Center was founded on the island, led by Rabbi Aharon Blasberg.

There exists in Aruba a small cemetery which contains the graves of early Sephardim. It is located on Boerhavestreat in the capital city of Oranjestad, and it is the only reminder of earlier Jewish settlements on the island. In the early 2000s, the congregation conducted a restoration project to preserve the headstones which are hardly legible, even though the oldest stone only goes back to 1857.[7]

Aruba is presently a self-governing territory under the Dutch crown.

---

[4] Emmanuel, op. cit., p. 532. The Emmanuels detail the mining of gold and phosphate on p. 531.

[5] Berkey, B. & V., "Jewish Presence in Aruba." Also letter from Martha E. Lichtenstein to author.

[6] Ibid.

[7] Emmanuel, op. cit., p. 531, N. 64. Rabbi Emmanuel found only eleven stones in the Aruba cemetery, the oldest belonging to Joel de Jacob Moreno, who died in 1857. See also Aruba Jewish Community Bulletin. The members of the Jewish community of Aruba have become active in preserving cemetery stones, as have other Caribbean communities. While I was on a trip to Aruba, I was with synagogue officials who were unable to locate the original Sephardic graveyard. Our taxi driver knew where it was, however, a tiny graveyard populated with only a few stones.

5
THE BRITISH CARIBBEAN

Jamaica

Nevis

Barbados

Trinidad-Tobago

The Bahamas

The British Caribbean: Jamaica

As warships of the British navy sailed into Jamaican waters towards Kingston harbor in 1655, they were led by Campoe Sabbatha, a *Marrano* Jewish pilot.[1] He may well have enjoyed a secret pleasure watching the English navy surrounding Spanish Men of War and ultimately defeating them. They were liberating his fellow *Marranos* from the island's Spanish rule. Thus Jamaica, the third largest island in the Greater Antillles, began its reign as one of England's great colonies.

Secret Jews had already been living in Jamaica under Spanish and Portuguese rule. One of the titles Columbus earned as a result of his discoveries was Duke of Jamaica. The title descended to the Admiral's great-granddaughter, who married a Portuguese nobleman from the house of Braganza. Under feudal law, the wife's ownership became that of her husband: he became Duke of Jamaica. Converted Jews settled in Jamaica and no Inquisition was permitted. The Portuguese *Conversos* lived apart from the Spanish Christians.

By the terms of the Spanish surrender to the British, all Spaniards were to leave Jamaica ... except the *Marranos*. Once the British wrested control from Spain, island Jews openly professed their religion and were permitted to remain.

Since the Spanish surrender of Jamaica and the Recife Diaspora occurred within months of each other, Brazilian Jews went to Jamaica, together with others from English and Dutch

---

[1] Roth, <u>History of the Marranos</u>, p. 289.

islands (mostly Dutch Jews who had left Recife earlier) quickly making Jamaica's Jewish community prominent in the Caribbean. Almost immediately, this group began planting sugar and other tropical crops. They were soon an important part of Jamaican society.[2]

Their numbers must have been relatively large. In 1699, the London Council of Trade and Plantation recommended that the island's governor be directed to decree that Jews:

"be not obligated to be in Arms on their Sabbath or other Solemn Feast, unless it be when an enemy is in view."

Island life being less formal than that of England, Jews were fairly integrated and a British historian commented that Jamaica had "no reason to repent of her liberality towards them." (Jews)[3]

While the main concentrations of Jews were in Kingston, Port Royal and Spanish Town, there have been as many as 21 separate communities flourishing throughout the island since 1655.[4] A synagogue was established in Port Royal, that infamous stronghold of Caribbean pirates, before 1692. In that year, an earthquake destroyed the city and a certain Mr. Heath remembered on that frightful day that:

> "I turned into Ye Jewe's street in order to get home when their Synagogue fell by my side."[5]

By 1735, there were already at least 800 Jews in residence in Jamaica. Despite their freedoms and a measure of openness not offered in Europe, Jamaican Jews were still unable to vote in public elections. Moses Delgado saw the injustice of this and on behalf of his co-religionists, worked hard to remedy these abuses. By 1831

---

[2] Silverman, Rabbi Henry P. "Jamaica Blends Ancient and Modern Judaism", London Jewish Chronicle. London. undated (circa 1966).

[3] Hooker, Rabbi Bernard, "United Congregation of Israelites," un-paginated (c. 1963).

[4] De Souza, Ernest H., "Pictorial: Some Aspects of Jamaican Jewry," p. 6.

[5] "Jamaica Blends."

Delgado's efforts were successful: all civil disabilities applicable to the Jewish community were repealed. It was 27 years before Jews in England would enjoy the same freedom. A silver tankard was presented to Delgado as a gesture of the community's appreciation. That tankard now rests in the synagogue at Kingston.[6]

By 1849, Jamaica's Jewish community had taken full advantage of its political freedom. Eight of the 47 members of the Island's legislature were Jewish, including the Speaker of the House. On *Yom Kippur* of that year, the legislature adjourned its session out of deference to the Jewish members who would not be able to attend to the business of legislation on that day. Less than 20 years later, the number of Jews in the Legislature had grown to 13.[7]

Jews have not only contributed to Jamaican agriculture, they have been important in politics, culture and business. Included in their accomplishments are:

- Kingston and other Jamaican cities have regularly had Jewish mayors;
- Jews have served on Jamaica's Privy Council (the High Court);
- Jews have been jurists and distinguished members of the Jamaican Bar;
- The Daily Gleaner, Jamaica's oldest and only daily newspaper, was founded by brothers Phineas and Jacob de Cordova in 1834 (Jacob de Cordova also laid out the street plans for Waco, Texas)[8] ;
- Sir Neville Ashenheim, a well-known politician, was Jamaica's ambassador to the United States during the years immediately

---

[6] "United Congregation."

[7] Ibid.

[8] Encyclopedia Judaica, 1978 ed. Vol. V., p. 1455.

following Jamaica's independence from Britain in 1962.[9] Sir Neville is a direct descendant of the de Cordova Brothers.

Interesting Aside:
Not only was Jacob de Cordova a founder of Jamaica's leading newspaper, he was also a Texas pioneer. He and another French Sephardic Jew, Henry "Tex" Castro, were active in encouraging settlers to come to Texas after the War of Texas Independence. Jacob and his brother founded two other publications: The Texas Herald and Southwestern America. Jacob De Cordova became a member of the Texas House of Representatives after Texas entered the Union. Born in 1808, Jacob de Cordova died in 1868.

From early times, when Abraham Henriques, Solomon de León, David López and other Jews owned large tracts of sugar and vanilla plantations, to the present, Jews have had a positive experience on this island. In fact, since the English took control of Jamaica and expelled all its Spaniards, Judaism has been the oldest organized religion practiced on the island.

Natural disasters, however, have destroyed at least six synagogues over the centuries. There remains just one in use in Jamaica today. It, too, was wrecked by an earthquake in 1907, but was rebuilt four years later. *Shaare Shalom* (Gates of Peace), the United Congregation of Israelites, was first built in 1885. It is located on Duke Street in downtown Kingston, about ten blocks from the waterfront.[10]

Like other Sephardic synagogues in the Caribbean, *Shaare Shalom* shares the tradition of spreading sand across its floors. The

---

[9] "Jamaican Jewry Has Few Prospects," (no byline), *London Jewish Chronicle*, March 20,1970. Not only was Sir Neville Jamaica's first Ambassador to the United States, he was a prominent businessman, a direct descendant of the de Cordovas, and major owner of the Daily Gleaner. Postal, B. and Stern, M: Tourists Guide to Jewish History in the Caribbean, p. 53.

[10] Hooker, Rabbi Bernard, "Pulpit in the Sun," London Jewish Chronicle, date unknown.

synagogue seats 600. Its Ark rests against the Eastern Wall and the *bimah* (reading lectern) stands in the center of the building. Instead of facing the Ark, congregants face the *bimah* from both sides.

Women were seated upstairs when services were conducted in the Orthodox ritual. The congregation now follows a more modified and liberal service, and women are seated beside men. Many of the ritual objects one sees here are taken from other, now defunct Jamaican synagogues, and are hundreds of years old.

Old cemeteries are scattered all across Jamaica. There are ten throughout the island, four in Kingston alone and one of them surrounds an abandoned synagogue. The cemetery at Hunts Bay, just outside downtown Kingston, is the oldest religious burial ground in Jamaica. It was restored in 1938 and is a National Monument controlled by the Jamaican National Trust. It contains tombstones dating back to 1672, but is being ravaged by tropical weather and undergrowth, as are the rest of the historic sites throughout the island and the Caribbean. Over a dozen other significant abandoned Jewish sites, including historic synagogues, community houses and individual homes are sprinkled throughout the island.[11]

During World War II, many Jewish refugees, mostly Poles, were sent from neutral Lisbon, Portugal to Jamaica. They were put up in a camp called Gibraltar II, near Kingston. Some of these refugees remained on the island, but most left after the War.[12]

Unfortunately, the Jewish population of Jamaica is slowly diminishing. From a community of over 1,000 in 1960, the number dropped to 600 just a decade later. There were about 300 members of this once powerful and venerable community remaining at the beginning of the 21st Century, all highly regarded by the government and the citizens of their island.

From 1967 the island had no rabbi, but a qualified religious leader, Ernest de Souza, had been active as the synagogue's reader

---

[11] De Souza op. cit., pp 4-6.

[12] Tartakower & Grossman, The Jewish Refugee Today, p. 437, 450-451. Also Wischnitzer, Visas to Freedom, p. 184.

for over 40 years.[13] In 2012, a rabbi was brought to the island but he has since left. A more recent addition to the Jewish scene in Kingston is a Chabad Center led by Rabbi Yaakov Raskin.

It is estimated that here are 200-400 Jewish residents of Jamaica in 2018.

---

[13] De Souza, E.H., letter written to author.

The British Caribbean:
Nevis

The once-active Jewish community of Nevis, which in the 18th Century comprised a fourth of its European population, is long gone from this tiny 36 square mile island.[1] There remains, however, solid evidence of its presence in this quiet corner of the Caribbean.

Blessed not only with fertile soil for sugar cultivation, Nevis also has hot springs that lured wealthy and upper-class Britons from across the sea to enjoy its warm therapeutic baths in the 18th and 19th Centuries.

Nevis was discovered by Columbus on his second voyage, and named by him. Because of the almost perpetual clouds covering its large central peaks, at over 3,000 feet, its mountains give the impression of being snow-covered. Nevis is, therefore, a corruption of *nieve*, the Spanish word for snow.

Sephardim from nearby islands went there in the late 17th Century. Records in Amsterdam's synagogue establish the presence of a synagogue on Nevis in 1684, verifying the existence of a Jewish community before that time.[2] Whether that building

---

[1] Address by the Hon. R. I. Bradshaw, J.P; Prime Minister of St. Christopher, Nevis, Anguilla, 25 February, 1971 at the re-consecration of the Jews' Burial Ground, Charlestown, Nevis. Bradshaw quoted a West Indian writer who states that in 1724, "Jews were still estimated to be a quarter of the population and doing more than their fair share of trade." Mr. Bradshaw expressed a hope that Jews would return to Nevis to the benefit of that island.

[2] Marsden-Smedley, H. "The Jews of Nevis". <u>London Jewish Chronicle</u>, August 15, 1969.

still stands was a question that for a long time remained unanswered, as we shall see.

In 1724, note was taken of the influence of Nevis Jews by an island minister. He reported to his bishop in London that 700 white Europeans lived in Nevis, of which a fourth were Jews who had their own synagogue. He went on to say that the Jews were well-accepted in the country, but in town they were "charged with taking the bread out of the Christian's mouths."[3]

Extant records, however, show that at least one Jew served as a jury foreman and others as witness to wills of Christians, attesting to the fact that they were accepted within the community. Solomon Israel served as co-executor of the estate of Bernard White in 1769, proof that Jews enjoyed the same civil status and responsibilities as their Christian neighbors.[4]

Jews's Lane, connecting the synagogue and cemetery, in Nevis.

---

[3] Ezratty, H. "Old Sephardic Cemetery Re-Consecrated in Nevis," Journal of Sephardic Studies, Yeshiva University, Vol. V, H.Y. 1971.

[4] Marsden-Smedley, op .cit.

The Jewish traders of Nevis sailed all across the Caribbean, engaging in commerce with St. Eustatius, Barbados, Curaçao, Surinam, St. Thomas and St. Croix. Nevis Jews journeyed to Newport, Rhode Island, New York, Holland and England. All these destinations had well-established Jewish communities and, indeed, many Sephardim were related by birth or marriage to Nevis families. Isaac Pinhiera traveled to New York, where he died in 1710 and is buried in the cemetery in Manhattan that belongs to New York's Spanish and Portuguese synagogue. The tiny cemetery is located at Chatham Square, now a part of New York's Chinatown. Pinhiera's family was registered in the 1707 census taken in Nevis.[5]

Jew's School, once believed to be the old synagogue, in Nevis.

---

[5] Conversations with Hester Marsden-Smedley, whom I had the pleasure to meet when she attended the ceremonies in Nevis. Marsden-Smedley is a lineal descendant of 18th century plantation owners. Her family has maintained contacts with the island through interest and property ownership. She has written much about Nevis, some of which I had read before we met.

The community built what for years was thought to have been a handsome brick synagogue with an outside stairway leading to the (now removed) woman's gallery. The building was believed to have been a synagogue; for centuries it was known by islanders as the Jew's school.[6]

The date of the building's construction was unknown. It was believed to have doubled as a schoolhouse, for it was in that school that young Alexander Hamilton, later to become George Washington's military aide and the first Secretary of the Treasury of the United States, was believed to have received his early formal education. Hamilton was taught Hebrew from an unknown female teacher of the community. It was the only school Hamilton could attend. Since he was the illegitimate son of a Scottish trader, the island's Anglican school refused him entry.

In 1993, a team of scholars from Brandeis University discovered what was believed to be a Jewish compound made up of a *mikve* and perhaps some other communal buildings surrounding the area of the Jew's School.

A narrow path leading from the old building to the Jewish cemetery in Charleston is known as Jew's Walk. Lush tropical vegetation and a stone wall flank it. The cemetery was re-consecrated in 1971, with a full ceremony sponsored by the Nevis government and the aid and funding of Mr. and Mrs. Robert Abrams of Philadelphia. They were encouraged by Rabbi Malcolm Stern, an authority on the genealogy of colonial Jewry of the United States and the Caribbean.

---

[6] When I first saw the building, I had the distinct feeling this was a synagogue. There is a niche on the eastern wall, which could have contained an ark. The building once contained an upper floor that could have been a woman's galley. The overgrown tropical path called Jews Walk led from the cemetery to this building, still called the Jews School. Although it never was a synagogue but merely a communal building or a school, I believed it belonged to the Jews. In 1998, what may be a *mikve* was found near the building. See Serviss, Naomi, "Reclaiming Jewish Past in Nevis." Latitudes, 1998. But my observations were wrong.

66

A LIST OF THE TOMBSTONES IN THE JEWS' BURIAL GROUND, NEVIS.

1. Abenduna, Ralph.

2. Abundiente, Abraham, alias Abraham Gideon — date of death "6 de Tisri do A°5450 (September 27, 1689).

3. Abundiente, Bathsheba, wife of Rehiel (alias Rowland Gideon) — date of death "Tuesday, the 28th of Ab, 5444" (August 20, 1684).

4. Arrobus, Hananiah or Ananiah — date of death January 25, 1729/30.

5. Cohen, Daniel — date of death January 29, 1703/4.

6. C————?, Daniel Mendes — date of death 28 Tamuz 5444 (1684).

7. De Mezqueto (Mesquita), Abraham Bueno — date of death 1715.

8. Gomes, Abraham Isquiao David — date of death February ————?

9. Lobatto, Abraham Cohen — date of death 1869/90.

10. Lobatto, Rachell Cahanet — date of death September 28, 1701.

11. Maniche, ————ter, date of death February 20, 1679.

12. Men(des?), ————uas, date of death November 1768.

13. Rezya, Ribca Levy — date of death 6 Shebat 5444 (1684).

14. Rezya, Rachel Levy — date of death (1688).

15. Rodrigues, Benvenida Cohen — date of death 5 Tishri 5445, December 3, 1684, aged nineteen years.

16. Rodrigues, ? Cohen — (this may be deciphered as Abraham).

17. Senior, ————? date of death 18 de (Fe)brauro 1709 (This was probably Jacob).

There is a fragment of a stone bearing the name "Arobus".

A List of the Tombstones in the Jews' Burial Ground, Nevis

Archaeological investigations of The Jew's School and the cemetery were made by Dr. Michelle Terrell, who has determined that the Jew's School is, in fact, an 18th Century manor house built some 100 years after the Nevis Synagogue existed. A cistern in the manor house had been erroneously believed to have been the community's *mikveh*.

Dr. Terrell located the real synagogue from old island documents describing its location in relation to other properties. The synagogue was closer to Jews Walk and the cemetery than previously thought.

Unable to excavate the site, since buildings now cover it, Dr. Terrell has, nevertheless, documented 60 Jewish families in this area, which once served as Nevis' Jewish quarter.

Modern testing procedures used by Dr. Terrell have verified at least 44 more unmarked graves in Georgetown's Jewish cemetery. An additional stone was found, raising the total now extant to 19 that can be seen. The earliest gravestone is dated 1679.[7]

Only 18 graves can still be identified in the cemetery, the earliest dating community to 1684. The re-consecrated cemetery makes a handsome addition to Charleston, which is one of the best-preserved colonial villages in the Caribbean.[8]

Family names on the stones, Bueno de Mesquita, Rezys, Rodriguez, Senior, Gomes and Abundiente, recall the presence of West Indian Sephardim. A stone wall built for the re-consecration, surrounds the 200 by 75 feet graveyard. Wrought iron gates, in the shape of the Tablets of the 10 Commandments, grace the entrance. The island government maintains the graveyard in good condition.

At the time of this writing, there was no Jewish presence on Nevis. In 2011, the population of this island was 11,000.

---

[7] Terrell, Dr. Michelle M., "A Brief History of the 17th and 18th Century Sephardic Jewish Community in Nevis, Leeward Islands, Eastern Caribbean". Pamphlet privately printed. Also, "The Historical Archaeology of the 17th and 18th Century Jewish Community of Nevis, The British West Indies." UMI Dissertation Services, Ann Arbor, Michigan, 2000. (PhD dissertation).

[8] Conversations and correspondence with Prof. Robert N. Zeitlin, Department of Anthropology, Brandeis University, Waltham, Mass. 1993.

The British Caribbean:
Barbados

Barbados was another prime beneficiary of the Recife diaspora. Located outside the wide arc of Caribbean nations forming the Windward Islands of the Lesser Antilles, Barbados is 21 miles long by 14 miles wide and lies to the west of St. Vincent on the Atlantic Ocean. Its soil is rich and still bears the fruits of sugar harvests.

In 1654, a significant number of Recife Jews appeared in Barbados, requesting permission to establish residence on the island. Because of a history of "No disturbance and behaving themselves civilly and confirming to the government of this island," the Jews were granted permission to reside in Barbados under the "Laws and Statutes of the Commonwealth of England and of this island relating to foreigners and strangers."[1]

By 1678, the community of 300 was large enough to summon a *Marrano* rabbi, Eliau Lopez, who was born in Malaga, Spain.[2] Less than 100 years later, there were two active synagogues in Barbados, one in Bridgetown and the other in Speightstown.[3] Another Spanish rabbi later came to Barbados. Abraham Izidro

---

[1] Cohen, op. cit., p. 144.

[2] Postal, B. and Stern, M, op. cit., p. 19.

[3] Cohen, op. cit., p. 144. The Speightstown synagogue was destroyed by fire in 1739, during an apparently anti-Semitic riot due to a misunderstanding. It was never replaced. I do not consider this as anything more than an isolated incident, rare in West Indian history and certainly not state-sponsored bigotry.

Gabay was accompanied by his wife. The Inquisition had earlier imprisoned both of them.[4]

The importance of Jewish migration to Barbados was the transfer of their knowledge of sugar cultivation, which they learned from their new experience in Brazil. This skill, together with the use of a new type of sugar mill developed by David de Mercado, catapulted Barbados into the world market as a leading and important producer of sugar and rum.[5]

Sugar was as economically significant in the 17th and 18th centuries as petroleum is today. Growing, milling and selling sugar were all part of a total process developed by Sephardim, much to the chagrin of English planters who were often not as skilled in those areas. The near monopoly, under which Spanish and Portuguese Jews grew, milled and marketed sugar, was offset by special taxes imposed upon them by the Barbados Council to "keep things even."[6]

Blessed with molasses, a by-product of sugar refining, Barbados was the first to distill and export rum to the rest of the world.

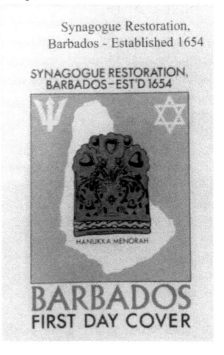

Synagogue Restoration, Barbados - Established 1654

SYNAGOGUE RESTORATION, BARBADOS-EST'D 1654

HANUKKA MENORAH

BARBADOS
FIRST DAY COVER

---

[4] Roth, History of the Marranos, p. 290.

[5] A Brief History of the Jewish Settlement in Barbados, no author, no date but predates final dedication of Nidhe Israel in 1987. Barbados Tourist Board, p. 3.

[6] Ibid, p. 3.

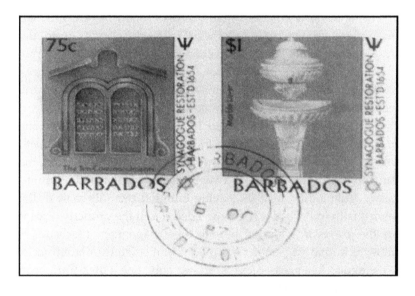

1987 Commemoration stamps showing interior and exterior of
Nidhe Israel Synagogue and some of its artifacts.

Synagogue *Nidhe Israel* (Scattered of Israel), built in Bridgetown in 1833, has been restored to its former beauty. The building is representative of the fluctuating fortunes of Barbadian Jewry in the past 200 years. Located at Synagogue and Magazine Lanes, *Nidhe Israel* was completed in 1833 to replace an earlier structure that had been almost completely destroyed by a hurricane in 1831. There has always been a synagogue on that site, commencing with the late 1600s. Not only Jews, but other distinguished members of Barbadian society and its clergy attended the 1833 dedication.[7]

Despite the handsome new religious home, the community's vigor began to abate because of the devastating effects of the 1831 hurricane and, later, by the decline of sugar in the world market which was caused by the abolition of slavery and the production of economically available sugar. By 1847, many Sephardim had immigrated to England, to other Caribbean islands, or to the United States. Only 71 Jews remained on the island.

In 1873, the Jewish population had declined to such a low point, the few congregants remaining successful petitioned the legislature for tax relief of the community's property.[8]

By 1900, only 17 Jews lived in Barbados. Nevertheless, one man, E.S. Daniels, ensured that the building was open for Sabbath prayer. Often he was the only worshipper. When Daniel died, the care of the property fell to two brothers, Joshua and Edmund Baeza. Joshua died in 1928, leaving Edmund the only male of the Jewish faith in Barbados. He proceeded to sell the property, except for the graveyards located next to the synagogue.[9] (Barbados is unusual in that its cemetery is placed immediately adjacent to its synagogue. As far as records show, only one other Caribbean synagogue, in Jamaica, followed this rare practice.)

---

[7] Bulletin, "The Barbados Jewish Community," *Shaare Tzedeck*, Bridgetown, 1992, unpaginated.

[8] Brief History..., op. cit. p. 9.

[9] Shilstone, op. cit., p. xxx-xxxii, (introduction).

The holy scrolls from the Barbados synagogue were sent to Bevis Marks, the Spanish and Portuguese synagogue in London, which also retained legal control over the cemeteries.

At public auction in 1934, the new owner sold the furniture and fittings that had not already been removed from *Nidhe Israel.* The synagogue became an office building with garages. Wooden storm shutters were torn from their frames. Arched windows were squared off and glass jalousies installed. The balustrade surrounding the roof was also removed, as was the canopy over the main entrance and the moldings surrounding the entrance to the second floor gallery. But the graveyards remained. They were intact, but not maintained, as had been solemnly agreed to in the deed of sale.

Barbados Synagogue as seen from the graveyard.

Almost simultaneously with the 1934 auction, new immigrants migrated to Bridgetown. They were Ashkenazic Jews from Central and Eastern Europe, motivated by Europe's political unrest. Others soon followed. Among the newcomers was the Altman family.

The Altmans were resolved to restore Jewish life to the island, and helped form Barbados Congregation *Shaare Tzedek*. Services were at first held in their home. When True Blue, an estate with a building was purchased, it was converted for use as a synagogue.[10]

Later, a community of black Jews was also established, called House of Zion. This congregation is made up of Barbadians who had lived in the United States and had contact with Jews there and became converted. Upon their return to Bridgetown, they formed their own congregation.[11]

The Barbados government purchased the old   synagogue in 1982, planning to demolish the building and erect a government facility. Community pressure, and a campaign to collect money to restore the building, resulted in the government deeding the building to the Barbados National Trust. The restoration was undertaken and on December 18, 1987, the building was rededicated.[12]

Restoration included the return from the Barbados Museum of an 1812 clock manufactured in London, and faithful reproductions of the synagogue's chandeliers, which had been sold to the

---

[10] Conversations with Paul Altman, community leader.

[11] Conversation with Marshall Oran, at the time President of *Nidhe Israel*. Oran related to me that *Nidhe Israel* assisted this congregation in matters such as arranging for *matzot* for Passover. In the May 1993 copy of "The Visitor," a tourist publication, a full page is listed for the island's religious institutions. In the section marked "Jewish," beneath *Nidhe Israel* appears the following listing: (I produce it exactly as it appears): "The Congregation of Zion House of Israel Congzhi, Neils Road, Haggatt Hall at St. Michaels. Saturday services. Shacrith service 11 a.m. every fourth shabbath. Minchag at 4 p.m. All feasts are observed. Call 429-2534 or 429-3020." Each time I have been in Barbados, I have been unable to attend a service there.

[12] Brief History..., op. cit. p. 10.

DuPont's Winterthur Museum in Delaware in 1934.[13] The museum, which had refused to sell the chandeliers, permitted artisans to photograph it so that a faithful reproduction could be made.

The special prayer book printed for the occasion states, "This service, the first to be held here after an interval of almost one-hundred years, is in honor of the British Commonwealth Jewish Council Conference."

The clock inside the Barbados Synagogue was manufactured in London in 1813.

The building, beautifully reborn, stands with its old cemeteries at the end of Synagogue Lane, just a block from Swan Street... once known as Jew Street. It was on that very street that the early Sephardim focused their commercial life during the 1600s, living above the shops where they transacted business.

---

[13] Conversations with both Marshall Oran and Paul Altman, who were among the moving forces behind the restoration. Much of the old furnishings were scattered throughout Barbados, many of them winding up in the Barbados Museum. Some of the original artifacts were returned. The handsome colonial chandeliers wound up in the Dupont Museum at Winterthur in Delaware. The Museum would not return the chandeliers. It would, however, permit artisans to take photographs and measurements, in order to duplicate them. The Oran family donated the reproduced chandeliers to the synagogue.

The story of the old synagogue and its gravestones can never be complete without recognizing Eustace M. Shilstone, a Barbadian lawyer who, fascinated with the stories the tombstones told, proceeded to record each and every one.

As a young man, Shilstone frequently walked past the abandoned graveyards. He became curious about the lives of the souls interred there. Shilstone was not Jewish, so he taught himself Hebrew as well as Spanish and Portuguese. Encouraged by the English and American Jewish Historical Societies, he published a book in 1955 called <u>Monumental Inscriptions in the Jewish Synagogue at Bridgetown, Barbados</u>. Complete with notes and the history of the Jewish community, it is a first-class work of scholarship, and each tombstone is documented with translations from its original languages.[14]

The cemetery contains, among many interesting graves, the remains of Rabbi Haim Carigal, who spoke at the Touro Synagogue in Newport, Rhode Island in 1772. It was the first American sermon ever given by a rabbi in Spanish and then published in the United States. Carigal, born in Palestine, traveled throughout the Americas and finally settled in Barbados. Spanish was Carigal's first language and that of many of Newport's congregants at the time.[15]

Graves of the relatives of Solomon Nuñes Carvalho are also in this cemetery. Nuñes Carvalho, who was born in Charlestown, South Carolina, lived for a time with an uncle in Barbados as a young man. He is best remembered for crossing the Rocky Mountains in 1853 with the famous Western explorer and U.S. Presidential candidate, John Charles Fremont. Nuñes Carvalho's paintings and photographs, and his written description of the expedition to the West as recorded in his dairies, were to become the major chronicles of Fremont's discoveries.

---

[14] Strouse, Samuel S. "He Learned Hebrew from Tombstone Inscriptions," <u>The Jewish Digest,</u> July 1970.

[15] Friedman, Lee M. <u>Rabbi Haim Carigal</u>. Private printing. Boston 1940.

This old gravestone belongs to Meir Cohen Belifanti, the *hazzan* and *mohel* of the community. He died in 1752. At the top, the hands in priestly blessing symbolize his being a Cohen, or high priest. At bottom, he is shown blowing a *shofar*, one of his duties as *hazzan*. His job as scribe is also commemorated, as are the tools of a *mohel* (circumciser), which he practiced. The gravestone is carved in Hebrew, Portuguese and English along the borders.

Old Barbados gravestone destroyed by an earthquake. The letters
SBAGDEG, which appear on many Caribbean gravestones is
Portuguese for *"Sua Bendita Alma Goze De Gloria,"*
(May his/her blessed soul enjoy glory."

Nuñes Carvalho was also a pioneer in early American photography, a portrait painter, and an inventor and writer. When he lived in Baltimore, Maryland, he and his wife founded a short-lived Sephardic congregation and one of the first religious schools in that city.

His uncle Emanuel was *hazzan* (cantor) of *Nidhe Israel* in 1798 and his father, David Nuñes Carvalho, was also active in synagogue affairs in the United States. There are several members of the Nuñes Carvalho family buried in the Nidhe Israel cemetery.[16]

Shilstone's dedication to his task and the publication of his book would have been enough to memorialize the role of the Jews in Barbados. But he did not stop there. Outflanked in his efforts to buy the property, Shilstone worked untiringly to have it put into the hands of the Barbados National Trust. He hunted down and located objects once used in the old building, and had them placed in the island's museum. Finally, he lobbied for and got permission to allow modern burials in the cemetery, whose oldest stone dates to 1660. Some current burials include that of a World War II Holocaust survivor. There are approximately 375 stones located in three graveyards. There may have been as many as five graveyards. Two cemeteries probably were lost to commercial use in the surrounding area.

Sorrowfully, Shilstone died in 1969, before he could see the synagogue restored.

The efforts of this man, a Gentile who understood the historic beauty of the old building and its decaying cemetery as things to

---

[16] Shilstone, <u>Monumental Inscriptions in the Jewish Synagogue at Bridgetown, Barbados</u> p. 101. Tombstone #256: Shilstone lists this historic tombstone as broken in five pieces. In Cohen, op. cit., p. 145, Rabbi Malcolm Stern states that many stones were removed from the ground and mounted on walls, to be lost forever. In Shilstone, op. cit., Carvalhos and Nuñes Carvalhos are listed with inscriptions (in alphabetical order) p., 72, 4, 299, 51, 67, 143, 85, 309, 305, 139. See also Sturhan, Joan, <u>Carvalho: Portrait of A Forgotten American,</u> Richwood Publishing Co., N.Y. 1976 and Ezratty, H., <u>They Led the Way: The Creators of Jewish America</u>, Omni Arts, Baltimore, MD. 1999, p. 89-100.

be preserved, testify to the good relations Caribbean Jews have always had with their Christian neighbors.

Today, visitors to Bridgetown can see a newly restored synagogue with a preserved and well-kept cemetery. The outside stairway leads to the upper women's gallery, as is typical of the West Indian Sephardic synagogues. The Barbados Synagogue does not have sand on its floors, as do other old West Indian synagogues. Its black and white checkerboard marble floor is the original set in in the 1833 construction. Using modern computer technology, enlargements of old photographs of the building were used in the restoration of *Nidhe Israel,* so that details of the interior could be faithfully reproduced.[17]

Nidhe Israel is open weekdays as a museum for visitors. On the Sabbath, it is given over to regular prayer. Because it has no air-conditioning, during the summer months the congregation meets at True Blue, formerly a private house in the suburbs, which for years was Barbados' only functioning synagogue. Known as *Share Tzedek,* it houses the community's religious school and library.

The Barbados Museum, in a 1942 publication, had the following to say about its early Jewish population: "The Jews of those days long ago, in spite of the disabilities imposed upon them, showed the Christians of the land how to succeed in the face of distressing odds. More than that, at a time when there was a slackness in living, and a weakness in morality, they, by their compact and organized manner of life, set a bright example of piety, of religious enthusiasm and of the security and sanctity of family life."[18]

---

[17] Conversations with Marshall Oran and Paul Altman. From photographs existing prior to its run down state, 20th century technology was able to identify all of the ritual objects so that they could be properly duplicated. Items such as the chandelier, *bimah,* ark and congregant's benches were all faithfully reproduced.

[18] Brief History..., op. cit. p. 11.

Barbados has no rabbi. Approximately 60 Jewish adults and 30 children live in Barbados. The island's population is 225,000, making it one of the world's most densely populated countries. In a conversation with Marshall Oran, one of the community leaders, he told me that the presence of the Jewish community and its numbers have remained static.

In 2002, the modern Museum of Barbados' Jewish history was opened on the synagogue grounds. It is a state-of-the-art museum with hands-on exhibits and is a beautiful facility.

The British Caribbean:
Trinidad-Tobago

Until the second decade of the 19th Century, Jewish settlements under Spanish control in Trinidad and Tobago were naturally restricted because of Inquisitional courts. Both islands were under the Bishopric of Cuba. Yet Sephardim did live here, hiding their true identities. They must have become assimilated since few, if any, Jews came forward after the English assumed control of Tobago from Spain in 1797 and Trinidad in 1818. This may be because Trinidad-Tobago fell to the British more than a century after most other Caribbean islands. While it remained in Spanish hands, *Marranos* were more likely to assimilate. Spanish is still spoken in Trinidad's mountain villages, however, attesting to the Hispanic influence that lingers on the island.

A small Jewish community did exist in Tobago late in the 17th century. Historians know that Daniel Levi de Barrios, the Poet Laureate of Amsterdam's Sephardic community, stopped at Tobago with a group of Jews on a colonizing trip to the Guyanas. It was here that his wife died from the ardors of the voyage. He returned to Amsterdam to become involved in the Sephardic community.

When de Barrios came to Tobago, it had been controlled by Latvia. Tobago is interesting because during the 1600s a part of the island was settled under the Latvian patronage of the Duke of Courland. The island was named New Courland and to this day there is a bay called Great Courland Bay.

Until the 20th century, there were no organized Jewish communities on either of these islands, which together total 1,979 square miles. The Barbados cemetery reveals, however, that at least one member of the community, Isaac Barber Isaacs, died in Tobago in 1964 and was returned to Bridgetown, Barbados for burial.

By World War I, a small number of Middle Eastern Sephardim and Central European Ashkenazim made Trinidad their home. Almost 20 years later, European turmoil brought approximately 2,000 Jews to the island seeking political and religious asylum. More Jews came during World War II. Because of its location just off the coast of Venezuela in the Southern Caribbean, Trinidad's importance as a military base brought American servicemen there to protect the Venezuelan oil fields.

During the late 1930s and the early World War II years, a formal congregation was founded. But with the steady erosion of the Jewish population after the War, all hopes of constructing a permanent community and synagogue were abandoned.

There is a cemetery at Mucurapo called *Bet Olam*, which contains recent graves. A trust fund was established for their perpetual care.

One interesting note: a housing complex called New Yalta was assembled out of swampland by a Jewish real estate developer. It is laid out with streets named for Jewish leaders, such as Herzl, Ben Gurion, Weitzmann, Einstein and Salk.[1]

Very few Jews remain in Trinidad-Tobago, but in 2018 a Chabad Center was established on the island, led by Rabbi Eli Chalkin.

---

[1] Postal, B. and Stern, M, op. cit. Much information regarding this island was gleaned from this book by Postal and Stern. See also Roth, History of the Marranos, p. 290 and pages 333-334 and the story of Daniel Levi de Barrios, who escaped from Portugal's inquisition and married Deborah Vaez in 1660. They sailed from Livorno (Leghorn) Italy to the Caribbean. Shortly after arriving at Tobago, Deborah died. Downhearted, de Barrios sailed back to the Continent, where he apparently returned to Christianity. He became a Captain in the Spanish Army and at the same time, a writer and poet and later a eulogist for the Amsterdam community, having been restored to Judaism. Also, Arbell, M. "*Daniel Levi de Barrios, poeta, dramaturgo I istoriador,*" Aki Yerushalayim, Kol Israel, Jerusalem, #15 special edition 1994.

The British Caribbean:
The Bahamas

Although it is not geographically part of the Caribbean, it is fitting that the island archipelago known as the Bahamas is included in this book. It was here that Columbus and his recently-converted Jewish interpreter Luis de Torres, made the first recorded landfall in the Western Hemisphere, on October 12, 1492.

Columbus, who named practically all the islands throughout the Caribbean, gave the name San Salvador to the first island he sighted. Today, it is known as Watlings Island.

Nassau, situated on New Providence Island, is less than 200 miles southeast of Miami. Freeport, on Grand Bahamas Island, is 65 miles east of Palm Beach.

Two 20th Century Jewish communities existed in the two main Bahamian cities of Nassau and Freeport until recently. Neither had links to any Spanish and Portuguese immigration. There is, however, a small walled-off section of Jewish graves in Nassau's public cemetery, which go back to the 19th century and contain Sephardic burial sites.[1]

Early settlement of these islands were sporadic and by English Jews, starting in the late 17th century, but with no establishments of any Jewish religious institutions. It was not until after World War II that Jews began settling in the Bahamas in significant numbers. The communities grew with the expansion of tourism. Two communities formed. One in Freeport, the Freeport Hebrew Congregation, follows the Reform ritual. It has another fitting

---

[1] Postal, B. and Stern, M, op. cit., p. 14.

name: The Luis de Torres Synagogue. This congregation meets in rented quarters and depends on tourists to maintain regular services, from High Holiday to Passover. It has about 16 resident families.[2]

On New Providence Island, the city of Nassau was home to another small congregation. The original organized community was the Conservative Nassau Hebrew Congregation, which was founded in 1965 and met in a space in a shopping center.[3] It gave way to a Reform Congregation and a new wave of Jewish families settling in the islands.

By the late 1980s and early 1990s, a new group of American residents began moving to the Bahamas. In 1996 they founded the Reform congregation known as the Bahamas Jewish Congregation.[4] This congregation grew from the needs of these newly settled young Americans who had migrated with their children, who required a Jewish education and preparation for Bar and Bat Mitzvah, including instruction in Hebrew. Their activity extended to the assistance of a student rabbi who made monthly visits to Nassau to help the community with its religious needs. In 1999, the Bahamas Jewish Congregation celebrated its first Bar Mitzvah, that of Brent Jaffe who, with the assistance of the visiting rabbi, led the congregation in prayers, including his *parasha* (a reading of the weekly portion of the *Torah*).[5]

The congregations banded together in 1997 to arrange for the release from a Bahamian detention camp of a Ukrainian Jewish family of four. They raised sufficient sums to support the family while their petition to enter the United States was being processed.[6]

---

[2] Letter of Jack Turner, President of Freeport Jewish Community, 1993.

[3] Rose, Harry, "The Bahamas Jewish Community,": Jewish Ledger, July 17, 1970.

[4] Conversations with Suzanne Jaffe Esfakis, resident of Nassau from 1991-2000.

[5] "Bahamas Jewish Congregation Celebrates First Bar Mitzvah," article Nassau Guardian, December 1999.

[6] Newsletters, 28-Jul-1977; 21-Aug-1977.

Some of the regular attendees at services are native Bahamians awaiting the opportunity to convert to Judaism.[7] Bahamians have long been interested in the Jewish religion. However, since there are no permanent rabbis in the islands, native Bahamians with a sincere interest in conversion must make the trip to Miami where they take instruction leading to conversion.[8]

The Luis de Torres Synagogue is the only remaining synagogue in the Bahamas. The number of Jews living there has fluctuates over the decades, of course, but was estimated at 300 in 2018. They are mostly professionals, business people and those involved in tourism. The current population of the Bahamas is approximately 293,000.

---

[7] Rose, Harry, op. cit.

[8] Suzanne Jaffe Esfakis; Faith Fovil, "Bahamas Jewish Congregation: Experience a Sense of Kehilah," Nassau Guardian, October 10, 1978.

6

The Danish & American Caribbean

St. Thomas

St. Croix

The Danish & American Caribbean: St. Thomas

This 27 square mile island located 40 miles east of Puerto Rico is part of the U.S. Virgin Islands. Originally a Danish colony, it was sold to the United States in 1917, together with St. Croix and St. John. These three islands make up the United States Virgin Islands.

The Virgin Islands has had three Jewish governors during its history. It is the only West Indian island with that distinction. The first, from 1684-1686, was Gabriel Milan, a *Marrano* who was removed by the Danish king and hung for "irregularities."[1] Later governors appointed by U.S. presidents were Morris Fidanque de Castro and Ralph Paiewonsky. They held office during the 1950s and 1960s with greater distinction than their predecessor.[2]

With such Jewish connections, one could correctly surmise that this island has had a long Jewish history. The Recife diaspora brought a small, unorganized group of *Marranos* to St. Thomas. They were mostly shopkeepers. Later, another misfortune led to St.

---

[1] Relkin & Abrams, <u>A Short History of the Hebrew Congregation of St. Thomas</u>, p. 22. Although Milan was a member of the influential *Marrano* families (da Costa and de Castro), he was apparently a rogue of the first order. Charged with consorting with pirates, he was recalled to Denmark for trial and subsequently executed. See also Cohen, op. cit., p. 153.

[2] Paiewonky, I., "Jewish Historical Development in the Virgin Islands 1665-1959," un-paginated [see calendar entry for 1950.] Fidanque de Castro, born in Panama in 1902, and registered in St. Thomas (at the time still a Danish colony) was appointed Governor by Harry S. Truman in 1950. Also, Relkin & Abrams, op. cit., p. 30. Ralph Paiewonsky was appointed governor of the Virgin Islands by John F. Kennedy in 1961 and served until 1969.

Thomas' first permanent and organized community. The Jews of St. Eustatius, never having recovered from losses inflicted by Admiral Rodney in 1781, began drifting to Curaçao and the North American mainland. In addition, a significant number came to St. Thomas. By 1796, a congregation called *Beracha V'Shalom* (Blessings and Peace) was flourishing. Early synagogues were located on Crystal Gade, which came to be known as Synagogue Hill.[3]

A succession of synagogues was built on the same site on this steep hill as each preceding one was destroyed by natural disasters. In 1833 the congregation erected its current, now well-known stone building, built to be both fire- and hurricane-proof. Soon the Jews of St. Thomas accounted for approximately half of the island's European population.[4]

Cemeteries at Savan and Altona testify to the strong Jewish presence in St. Thomas for over two centuries. Some of the stones are so weatherworn they can no longer be read. Others, carved in Portuguese, Spanish, Hebrew, English and French, tell the story of the movements of Sephardim from within the Caribbean to the United States, France, Holland, England, Denmark and Germany. A street near the old cemetery at Savan still bears the Danish name, *Joden Gade* (Jew Street) to remind us that Jews probably congregated in this neighborhood centuries ago.[5]

Much of the prosperity enjoyed by early Sephardim was conducted by sugar cultivation, rum, shipping and trade. With the abolition of slavery, the decline of sugar, and later, with the eclipse of the sailing ship, St. Thomas became a seldom-visited island. Its Jews left for the United States, Curaçao and fresh opportunities in Panama that arose from the newly constructed Canal. Among the families that left for Panama were the de Castros, Robles and the Sassos.

---

[3] Woods, Edith de Jongh, The Royal Three Quarters of the Town of Charlotte Amalie, Mape Mondes Ltd. U.S.V.I. 1992, p. 64.

[4] Jewish Historical Development, pp. 19 and 24.

[5] Margolinsky, J.,"299 Epitaphs in the Jewish Cemetery in St. Thomas; W.I.," The Royal Three Quarters, p. 133.

Despite the fact that few Jews remained in St. Thomas, the synagogue remained in use and was available for prayer every Sabbath. The community maintained a rabbi to perform regular religious services. Rabbi Moses Sasso, who acted as the community's spiritual leader during this time, is a legend in St. Thomas for the 61 years of service he rendered as the community's spiritual leader.[6]

The entrance to the St. Thomas Synagogue, *Beracha V'Shalom,*
which is the oldest continuously-used synagogue in the United States.

---

[6] Postal, B. and Stern, M, op. cit., p. 70.

In 1917, when Denmark sold its islands to the United States, there were barely 100 Jews living in St. Thomas, a remarkable decline from the more than 400 who lived on the island 80 years earlier. During World War II, their numbers dwindled to a precarious 50.[7]

Thanks, however, to a vital tourist economy that has grown from 1960 to the present, as well as St. Thomas' status as a free port, Jews have returned to this beautiful island. Most of them have come from the United States, establishing free port shops and other businesses.

They pray at *Beracha V'Shalom*, the oldest synagogue in continuous use under the United States flag. It follows the tradition of other Caribbean synagogues with floors covered with sand. It also adheres to the Sephardic arrangement of Ark, *Bemah* and congregational seating.[8]

Unlike most Caribbean Sephardic synagogues however, *Beracha V'Shalom* is only one story high. During the years that it followed the Orthodox Sephardic ritual, women sat apart from men, but only one step up. The Congregation now follows Reform ritual.[9]

Among its treasured religious objects are a *menorah* which dates back to Spain and is 900 years old, and its famous antique Chair of Elijah, used in the circumcision of newborn males. In addition, some of its *Torahs* are centuries old.

The Congregation maintains up-to-date social and educational facilities in a separate building across the narrow road from the Synagogue. Unfortunately, that facility was almost completely destroyed during Hurricane Marilyn in 1995. It has since been rebuilt and functions once again as a social center for island Jewry.

---

[7] Ibid, p. 70.

[8] "La Nación,: The Spanish and Portuguese Jews in the Caribbean," Museum of the Jewish Diaspora, Tel Aviv, un-paginated.

[9] "St. Thomas of Yesteryear," letter of David Stanley Sasso, congregant, St. Thomas Congregation's Newsletter, March 1993.

Throughout its long history, the St. Thomas Jewish community has given leaders to both the United States and the world. It was here that Camille Pissarro was born and spent his childhood. Sent to be educated in France, he returned to St. Thomas but left once again to satisfy his love for painting and his attraction to Paris. Pissarro became not only a leading painter of the Impressionist School; he was a father figure and mentor to many of the great Impressionists. In 1996-97, the St. Thomas synagogue mounted an exhibit of early Pissarro art works, all of which had been executed in St. Thomas during the 1850s.[10]

David (Levy) Yulee, born in St. Thomas in 1810, was a Congressman and later United States Senator from Florida. Since Yulee became a convert and denied he was a Jew (he claimed to be the son of a Moroccan prince), the distinction of being the first admitted Jewish Senator belongs to Judah P. Benjamin of St. Croix, who was elected to the U.S. Senate from Louisiana in 1853. Neither Benjamin nor Yulee could escape their religious past. On at least one occasion, fellow Senator (later president) Andrew Johnson denounced them on the Senate floor for their Jewishness.[11]

During the 1860s, General Antonio Lopez de Santa Ana, once ruler of all Mexico, conqueror of the Alamo and Sam Houston's foe and adversary in the Texas War of Independence, spent one of his many exiles in St. Thomas. He would sit dockside and tell all who would listen of his exploits and about the famous battle in which

---

[10] The St. Thomas Jewish community mounted a Pissarro exhibit in 1996 of watercolors executed by the artist after he returned from school in Paris and before his final return to France.

[11] Evans, Judah P. Benjamin: The Jewish Confederate, p. 261; Rosen, R, The Jewish Confederates, Univ. of South Carolina Press, 2000. See chapter 2 titled "Two Sephardic Senators," which details the lives of these two West Indian-born Jews who were influential in the South and were prominent in the Southern succession. Moses Levy, Yulee's father, may at one time have been a partner with Judah P Benjamin's father in the Virgin Islands. Moses Levy, a religious Jew, was one of the first to colonize Florida. His goal was to create a Jewish haven. Much of the acreage he purchased was later the power base for the political ambitions of his son, David Levy Yulee and for his dreams of a commercial empire complete with a railroad line and steamship company.

he lost his leg. One wonders whether he chatted with the Sephardic *hildagos* of St. Thomas in Spanish. Not only did they share a similar Spanish heritage but, at that moment of history, they had the same home in the middle of the Caribbean Sea.[12]

St. Thomas' Jews are found at all levels of the island's commerce and society. They are the proud custodians of their venerable synagogue and in 1996, celebrated the 200th anniversary of the establishment of their congregation.

The first Sephardic cemetery in St. Thomas.
The Hebrew dates 5510-5596 correspond to 1749-1835.
The man in the foreground (circled) is former
St. Thomas Rabbi Joseph Karasic who, with the author,
was recording gravestones in 1971.

---

[12] Michener, James, The Eagle & The Raven, T. Douherty, N.Y. 1990, p. 185.

Approximately 65 Jewish families lived in St. Thomas at the end of the 20th Century, down from 125 ten years earlier. The depletion is the result of two devastating hurricanes: Hugo in 1989 and Marilyn in 1995. However, the congregation is committed to having the services of a rabbi.[13]

Once, in times past, Crystal Gade, or Synagogue Hill, was home to the families of *La Nacion*: Mendez-Monsantos, de Mordechays; Mottas; Henriquez; Nuñez; d'Azevedos; Levy Maduros; Pardos; Hohebs; Cardozes, and others. In the 21st Century, St. Thomas is home to Jews mostly of Ashkenazic descent.[14]

About 150 tourists visited the synagogue on Crystal Gade daily, most of them arriving via cruise ship. Those who ask island residents for the location of the Synagogue will almost always be given directions, as it is a landmark known by most St. Thomians.

A Chabad Center was opened at Red Hook Plaza led by Rabbi Asher Federman.

The overall population of the U.S. Virgin Islands has decreased slightly in the past decade, hovering at 105,000 in 2020.

---

[13] Conversations with current (2001) Rabbi Jay Heyman.

[14] Woods, op. cit., p. 51.

The Danish & American Caribbean: St. Croix

Settled before St. Thomas, St. Croix' Jews first banded together formally in the town of Christiansted in 1760. The former French island, with its racist *Code Noir*, would have been inhospitable to Jews but in 1733, the Danes took possession of St. Croix, after purchasing it from the French.

Danish religious policy was more liberal than that of France and attracted Jewish settlers to the island. But the community was unable to prosper. They did have a synagogue, which has long disappeared. A small cemetery, however, still remains in Christiansted, its stones spanning the period from 1779 to 1862. By the end of the 19th century, that early community was almost entirely disbanded.[1]

During its brief Jewish history, St. Croix was the birthplace of Judah P. Benjamin, one of America's greatest lawyers and a leader of the breakaway South during the Civil War. Benjamin was also Senator from Louisiana from 1853 to 1861. He turned down nominations to the U.S. Supreme Court and an Ambassadorship to Spain. Had he accepted either post, he would have been the first Jew to be so honored.

He was Attorney General and later, Secretary of State and Secretary of War in Jefferson Davis' Confederate government: he was often called "the brains of the Confederacy." Benjamin's political career was probably the most active and powerful of any Jew in American history.[2]

---

[1] Postal, B. and Stern, M, op. cit., p. 68.

[2] Evans, op. cit., p. xi (prologue).

The brilliant Benjamin escaped to England after the Civil War to start a new life. Assuming British citizenship, he became one of England's great barristers and authored <u>Benjamin on Sales,</u> still a classic legal text.

Benjamin's Marrano family traces their ties to St. Eustatius, where his grandmother, Hannah Benjamin de Leon, was a well-known medical practitioner, dispensing folk medicine to islanders. Her house was used as a synagogue when *Honen Dalim* was damaged during the hurricane of 1772.[3] Her tombstone rests in the Jewish cemetery in St. Eustatius.[4]

The name Judah Benjamin appears as one of the St. Eustatius synagogue directors in 1772. This Benjamin was probably a close relative of Judah P. Benjamin of St. Croix, since Sephardim follow the tradition of perpetuating names from generation to generation, even among the living.[5]

According to folklore, one of St. Croix' Jewish community, Christina Levine, married the notorious pirate Jean Lafitte, and died aboard one of his ships in 1804. Lafitte himself appears to have been Jewish.[6]

---

[3] Ibid. p. 3

[4] Emmanuel, I. and S, op. cit., p. 1059. The inscription of Hannah Benjamin de Leon's headstone is set forth as it appears in the St. Eustatius cemetery.

[5] Ibid. pp. 520, 1058

[6] Saul, M., "*Pirates I Korsarios Djudios,*" <u>Aki Yershalayim,</u> Jan 2000, p. 62. Saul maintains that the Lafitte brothers were Jewish. After having devised an ingenious plan in league with the Spanish navy, the brothers then double-crossed them. Later, Lafitte issued orders not to attack American shipping in the Gulf of Mexico, only Spanish. Saul claims Lafitte had a vengeance against the Spaniards. "*en una sierta muzira, de los ke avian kavzado a su pueblo tantas sufriensas*" [with certain satisfaction against those who caused his people so much suffering]. One of Lafitte's biographers, Lyle Saxon, in <u>Lafitte the Pirate,</u> Pelican Pub. Co., Gretna (reprint) 1989, p. 68, 282-283, states that Lafitte had a lifelong vendetta and hatred for the Spaniards because they mistreated him during his imprisonment, p. 286. (Note that the article written by Saul is not in Spanish, but in Ladino, the language of the Sephardic diaspora.)

Never as numerous nor as active as the Jews of St. Thomas, Cruzan Jews have, however, undergone a minor resurgence in recent years.[7] They have their own synagogue and rabbi.

However, in September 2017, Hurricane Maris hit St. Croix and destroyed much of the island.

Currently, approximately 30 Jewish families reside in St. Croix. *B'Nai Or,* the synagogue that serves the St. Croix Jewish community, closed for the duration of the Coronavirus in April of 2020. They are using virtual approaches to maintain their connection with the congregation and will reassess their situation later in the year.

---

[7] Conversations with Alan Bronstein, president of Cong. *B'nai Or,* St. Croix, U.S.V.I.

7

THE SPANISH CARIBBEAN

Puerto Rico*

Cuba

The Dominican Republic

* Puerto Rico is a Freely Associated Commonwealth within the
United States, but is here listed as Spanish because of its early and
long history as a colony of Spain.

The Spanish Caribbean: Puerto Rico

Although Puerto Rico, the fourth largest island in the Greater Antilles, is currently home to the largest Jewish population of any Caribbean island, it was not always so. The Recife diaspora of 1654, which enriched most Jewish life in the West Indies, had no effect on Puerto Rico.

Unlike Dutch, Danish and British islands that are rich with Jewish memories and monuments, Puerto Rico has no significant records of any settlements, synagogues or cemeteries existing before the 20th century. As a Spanish island until 1898, it was an inhospitable place for Jews because of Spain's laws banning Jewish settlement and the immigration of converted Jews until the fourth generation in her territories, and the establishment of Courts of Inquisition.

At the beginning of the 21st Century however, the Jewish population of Puerto Rico was approximately 2,000. The island, 110 miles long by 45 miles wide and located at the southeastern end of the Greater Antilles, had a total population of almost four million and the most significant and active Jewish community in the Caribbean.

Interesting Aside:

Over the past 32 years, the Jewish community has tried to verify the actual number of Jews on the island. Members of *Shaare Tzedek* (Conservative) number approximately 225 families, which is about 1,000 individuals. Members *of Beth Shalom* (Reform) number approximately 85 families, or 350 individuals. The rest of the numbers, which have never been substantiated, come from non-affiliated Jews who are well-known in the tourist industry, manufacturing, transportation, educators at the universities, civil servants, etc. and Jews around the island who have intermarried and only make their presence known during High Holidays, crises such as the 1967 and 1973 Israeli Wars, or respond to island-wide requests for fund raising. Included in this grouping are Israelis engaged in agriculture outside San Juan, who are for the most part unaffiliated. Another unaffiliated group is the 'snowbirds,' Jews from the mainland who spend the winter season in San Juan.

The presence of more Jews on the island surfaces when a Christian spouse seeks a Jewish burial for a dead partner or someone calls to request a Jewish wedding for his or her child entering into an interfaith marriage.

Based on educated guesses, it had long been estimated that there were between 2,000 and 2,500 Jews living in Puerto Rico. By 2019, the number changed to 1,500.

Three synagogues are maintained in Puerto Rico, only one with a full time rabbi. Many Jewish support organizations from the American mainland maintain chapters on the island.

There are sparse records of some Jews having lived in Puerto Rico during the Spanish colonial period. From what historians have been able to ascertain, there were no organized Jewish settlements, just individual Sephardim with Spanish family names, who were familiar with Hispanic culture and language. They came mostly from Curaçao and Venezuela.

Sarah Nuñes Mercado died in Guayanilla in 1805. Elias de Sola lived in that same town in 1839. Isaac de Lima practiced medicine in Mayagüez in 1840; Solomon Senior died in Aguadilla in 1849 and was taken to Curaçao for burial. There is also a history of one Judah Cohen of Curaçao having been killed by Spaniards in Puerto Rico in 1723. Cohen appears to have been a merchant trading illegally in Spanish territory.[1]

---

[1] Emmanuel, I. and S, op. cit., p. 83, 347, 835.

It was not until 1898 that Jews came to Puerto Rico in significant numbers and without fear of running afoul of Spanish authorities. The United States had defeated Spain in the Spanish-American War, thereby gaining control of both Cuba and Puerto Rico. American Jewish servicemen and administrators soon arrived. No formal community arose, however, as servicemen remained only a short while and most administrators left after completing their tasks.

Jewish administrators did much to assist Puerto Rico form the establishment of the island's legal and fiscal codes, and create and staff its court system. Among them were Louis Sulzbacher, Adolph Wolf and Cecil Snyder, the latter who became Chief Justice of Puerto Rico's high court.[2] Later, during the decade of the 1960s, the law School at the University of Puerto Rico was led by the Harvard educated Dean, David Helfeld, who educated a generation of lawyers. Jewish public health officials began the process of ridding Puerto Rico of its tropical diseases. Among them were William Hoffman and Charles Weiss.

Interesting Aside:

The legal profession in Puerto Rico has been enriched by the presence of members of the Jewish faith. Max Goldman, product of a religious education in New York, came to the island at the behest of the legendary Governor Muñoz Marin. Muñoz spearheaded "Operation Bootstrap" and Goldman was closely associated with the island's tax exemption law, which spurred the arrival to the island during the 1950s and 1960s of manufacturers and managers (including many Jews).

One of Puerto Rico's outstanding trial lawyers, Harvey Nachman, a native of Saratoga Springs, New York, flew with the Israeli Air force during the War of Independence in 1948. Everyone, Christian and Jew, knew Harvey to be an indefatigable collector of money for Israel. His strong impact on the legal profession was recognized by his colleagues: Harvey Nachman was the quintessential model for Puerto Rican

---

[2] Acosta, Velarde, Federico, _El Primer Tribunal Supremo de Puerto Rico_, San Juan, Puerto Rico, 1940, p. 26, and Carrion A., Puerto Rico: A Political and Cultural History, W.W. Norton & Co., N.Y. 1983, p. 235, 264.

lawyers for almost four decades. When he died, the law library in the Federal District Court was dedicated to Nachman's memory. At his funeral, judges, lawyers, clients and friends of all religions paid their respects. His coffin was draped with three flags: those of the United States, Israel and Puerto Rico.

Not until the beginning of the First World War did large numbers of Jews return to the island. After that War, the island's Jewish population waned again. Then, during the late 1920s and early '30s, Jews from Central and Eastern Europe immigrated to Puerto Rico. American Jews came too, as representatives of mainland interests such as the Consolidated Tobacco Company.[3]

Early settlers engaged in business and merchandising. Aside from informal gatherings on religious holidays and other special occasions, there was no functioning Jewish community. In 1927, the tiny community numbered only 27 families.[4]

It was during World War II that the Jewish community increased substantially. Servicemen and military rabbis arrived. Lavy Becker and Bertram Pollans held regular services with civilians also attending. They became actively involved with the community. At the close of W.W. II, the servicemen and rabbis left, but the War years had strengthened the permanent Jewish community and its resolve to grow.

The Jewish Community Center (JCC), as the congregation was first known, purchased a private home in 1953 and converted it into a synagogue. In 1959, Puerto Rico had 200 Jewish families. By 1967 the JCC, also known as Congregation *Shaare Tzedek* (Gates of Mercy) had to enlarge its facilities. The basically American-oriented congregation had received an influx of Jewish exiles from Castro's revolution in Cuba. These refugees enriched the growing community not only with their numbers, but also with dedication to their religion.[5]

---

[3] Postal, B. and Stern, M, op. cit., p. 60-61.

[4] Ezratty, Barbara Tasch, Puerto Rico An Oral History 1898-2008, Read Street Publishing, Baltimore MD, 2009.

[5] Ibid. p.186.

Interior of Temple *Beth Shalom*, the Reform Jewish Congregation of
Puerto Rico at Calle San Jorge. Local architect Tom Marvel incorporated
the Caribbean look for the sanctuary, remodeled in the late 1980s.

Successive generations of the Cuban families have given a Hispanic orientation to *Share Tzedek's* services. Although there is currently no rabbi, a *hazzan* performs services. The use of a *hazzan* has been a time-honored means for Caribbean and Colonial American Jews to continue prayer services when no rabbi was available.

Many congregants were executives and employees of Jewish-owned businesses established on the island after "Operation Bootstrap" was inaugurated. "Operation Bootstrap" was a successful effort by the government to bring manufacturers to the island by granting tax and other economic incentives. Closely allied to the drafting and implementing of this plan was Max Goldman, a U.S. mainland attorney who relocated to San Juan during the 1950s. Jews fit well into Puerto Rican society.[6]

Another group of American Jews, many of them professionals, educators, managers and civil servants, formed a second congregation on the island with the assistance of the Union of American Hebrew Congregations (UAHC) in New York. They became affiliated with the UAHC in 1967 under the name Reform Jewish Congregation of Puerto Rico. A few years later, the students in its religious school suggested the name by which it is more commonly known, Temple *Beth Shalom* (House of Peace.)

Worshipping at first in borrowed quarters, including a church and private homes, the congregation was finally able to rent a building directly across the street from *Shaare Tzedek*. Then, in 1971, they purchased their own home in the Condado section: a commercial building that once housed a bar. Only minimal funds were available for its conversion into a synagogue.

---

[6] Staub, M., "Puerto Rican Jews: A Cultural Mélange," <u>Sun-Sentinel</u>, May 1, 1998.

Interesting Aside:

Temple *Beth Shalom's* building was purchased in 1971 from the estate of a deceased businessman. The present location of the sanctuary was once a bar called "The Tenth Inning Lounge," owned by Rudy Hernandez, a one-time pitcher for the old Washington Senators. The rest of the building was given over to a pastry shop, a store selling woman's lingerie, and a soda shop. The second floor was occupied by tenants in four apartments. The author was assigned the task of handling negotiations with others for the purchase of the building and eviction of the commercial tenants, all of whom had stopped paying rent to the estate. Needless to say, lengthy litigation ensued, during which the commercial tenants refused to pay rent to the new owner. I spent much time in Court to resolve these problems.

By 1973, the Congregation moved into its new home after minimal renovations. Within two decades, it completed extensive renovations, including the removal of two apartments on the second floor to heighten the ceiling in the sanctuary (see photo in this section.)

When the congregation was first formed, its leased quarters were inadequate for the numbers wishing to attend High Holiday services. The Union Church graciously offered the use of their building without rent. The Church also permitted a pulley system that dropped a cloth to cover a crucifix approximately 6 to 8 feet high on the wall where the congregation placed its portable Ark.

During the 1980s, both congregations embarked upon extensive renovations of their respective buildings, emphasizing their strength and commitment to a Jewish future on the island.

Shaare Tzedek in the Miramar section of San Juan, boasts lush grounds and a building with an historical past: it was originally designed by the prominent Puerto Rican architect Nicodemas in the early 1900s. Renovations have retained the character of the old building while adding space for the congregation's large religious school.

Beth Shalom's renovation, under the direction of well-known local architect Tom Marvel, has changed its former Spartan quarters – there were some who once referred to it as "the storefront congregation" – into a comfortable and comforting sanctuary, similar in mood to the famous *El Transito* synagogue in Toledo, Spain. Schoolrooms, offices and a library on the upper floor form part of the synagogue complex.

One feature of *Beth Shalom's* experience is the many Puerto Ricans claiming a *Marrano* heritage who attend services. Several Puerto Ricans, including whole families, have undergone rabbinic conversion.[7]

Until 1996, the Temple's religious committee of lay leaders provided weekly services, bringing a rabbi from the U.S. mainland for High Holiday services and special events. Rabbi Albert Shulman was the first in 1967; Rabbi Gary Bretton-Granatoor conducted High Holiday services at *Beth Shalom* for ten years from 1985 to 1995, with Amy Dattner as cantor. She continued in that role until 2014. Rabbi Mordechai Rotem, the first Reform rabbi ordained in Israel, began his four-year association with *Beth Shalom* in 2001.

Throughout its history, *Beth Shalom* has focused on continuing Jewish education for its adult members. It has a reputation for bringing leaders of the Reform movement to the island to speak, has hosted the first female Reform rabbi ordained in the U.S, and has welcomed a variety of other lecturers. It also employed the first female rabbi to serve a congregation in the Caribbean.

The congregation now employs the services of retired rabbis for religious holidays and other occasions, or for months at a time. There are also scholars-in-residence for weekends or even weeks

Today, most of the congregants are local Jews-by-Choice, encouraging Spanish and Hebrew services on Saturdays. English and Hebrew are used more often at Friday night services.

Puerto Rico presently maintains three synagogues: Reform, Conservative and, since 1999, a Chabad Learning Center with a

---

[7] The conversion of many Puerto Ricans, including whole families, is a phenomenon that has occurred during the last few decades. Some families allege a Jewish past, together with remembrances of elderly relatives lighting candles on Friday evenings, etc. The growth of the crypto-Jewish population is being studied by the Society for the Study of Crypto Judaism; the study encompasses the southwest United States and most of Latin America.

full-time rabbi attendant. Rabbi Mendle Zarchi has been instrumental in overseeing the growth of the Chabad community. Rabbi Zarchi was the first rabbi in the Chabad movement to settle in the Caribbean. He and his wife came to Puerto Rico in 1998.

In early 2005, the Chabad Welcome Center was opened in a two-story space next to a jewelry shop in Old San Juan, just blocks from the seaport and ever-arriving cruise ships. The space was donated by the Demel family, owners of the shop and members of the Chabad congregation. Tourists were encouraged to stop into the Welcome Center for bottles of cold water, maps of the city, a small shop with Jewish-related souvenirs (including this book) and miscellaneous information about the island. The shop was run by Rabbi Levi Stein, when he was not assisting Rabbi Mendle at the synagogue. The Chabad movement has its new synagogue in the Isla Verde neighborhood, not far from the Luis Muñoz Marin International Airport.

There are only a few Sephardim among Puerto Rico's Jews, but the Spanish language is used by most of the community. *Shaare Tzedek's* services are conducted mostly in Spanish and Hebrew; *Beth Shalom* recognizes its Hispanic members by having mostly Spanish and Hebrew services on Saturdays with more English in the Friday night service.

The island's population has decreased significantly in the past decade, due to two natural disasters: the huge Hurricane Maria in 2017 and the devastating earthquakes of 2019 and 2020. *Beth Shalom* had been scheduled to celebrate its 50th Anniversary in late 2017, but the damage to its synagogue prevented a gathering. (It was the first time in its history that it missed a Friday night service.) Thanks to a committed congregation, with the help of the Puerto Rican community at large, extensive repairs were completed in the spring of 2018 and the celebration held then.

The Jewish population on the island is now estimated to be 1,500.[8]

---

[8] World Population Review, 2020.

The Spanish Caribbean: Cuba

The island of Cuba is 750 miles long. It is the largest and most populous island in the Caribbean and spreads from close to the American mainland to the northwest corner of Haiti. It is like Puerto Rico, however, in that it does not have a rich history of Jewish connections.

Among Cuba's first European settlers was Luis de Torres, the Jewish interpreter who had been baptized just before sailing with Columbus. As interpreter on that first voyage of discovery, de Torres was sent by the Admiral into the island's interior to find the Grand Khan, leader of the Asians that Columbus was seeking. Instead, during his march inland de Torres met natives smoking tobacco. After his voyage with Columbus, de Torres returned to the island and became the first European tobacco farmer. It is said he also negotiated a treaty between Columbus and the natives.[1]

Under Spanish rule, Cuba was a hostile environment for Jewish colonization. To settle there, Jews would of necessity have had to conceal their true religion. Such intrepid settlers who tried to do that, however, were often caught and dealt with harshly by the Inquisition, which was well-established in the New World, especially in Cuba, which was a Bishopric See and center for the Inquisition. Nevertheless, many converted Jews came secretly as settlers.

---

[1] Kayserling op. cit., p. 93-94.

Until 1898, when the United States acquired Cuba as a result of the Spanish-American War, no formal Jewish communities existed on that island. There were, however, some Jewish connections.

Stamp honoring Cuban-Jewish hero, Major General Carlos Roloff. When he was treasurer of Cuba, his signature appeared on Cuban bonds and other financial instruments.

In his quest for the island's independence in the decades before 1898, the Cuban patriot José Marti sought and received help from Floridian Jews during his years of exile in the United States. When America took control of the island, these mainland Jews were among the first settlers in Cuba. Shortly after the beginning of the 20th Century, they organized the island's first synagogue, The Union Hebrew Congregation, which followed the Reform ritual. [2]

**Another stamp honoring Cuban-Jewish hero,
Major General Carlos Roloff.**

---

[2] The Union Hebrew Congregation, following the Reform ritual, was the first synagogue established in Cuba in 1904. It was founded by Americans and no longer exists, having closed its doors during the 1980s.

Cuban historian Maritz Corrales has told this author that she believes José Marti to be a descendant of Crypto-Jews who settled in Cuba during the 1600s.[3] Indeed, the name Marti is found on the island of Mallorca and is well-known to be exclusive to Jews forcibly converted in 1391. These people are known as *Chuetas*.[4]

During the struggle for independence, at least one Jew maintained a position of prominence with Marti's revolutionaries. Carlos Roloff, a Polish-born naturalized American, found his way to Cuba to become one of Marti's trusted officers He attained the rank of general, while living as a guerilla in the Cuban forest. Upon achievement of Cuban independence, Roloff became Treasurer-General of Cuba and his name appeared as signatory on Cuba's 100 peso bonds issued in 1905.[5]

After Cuba was granted independence by the United States, Sephardic Jews from Curaçao, Turkey, Syria and other Levantine countries came to Havana, attracted by Cuba's opportunities and common language. By the 1920s and early '30s, a wave of Ashkenazic Jews, escaping European antisemitism, enlarged the community.[6] On the eve of Castro's Revolution in 1959, Cuban

---

[3] The Chosen Island: Jews in Cuba. Salsido Press, Chicago, IL, 2005.

[4] Moore, Kenneth, Those of the Street: The Catholic Jews of Mallorca, Univ. of Notre Dame Press, Indiana, 1976. The book details the exclusively Jewish family names of Mallorca, the Marti family name included.

[5] Millis, W., The Martial Spirit, Liberty Guild of America, N.Y. 1931, p. 31. See also this chapter, with postage stamp honoring Roloff.

[6] Tartakower & Grossman, op. cit., p. 92, 97, 206 (detailing the curtailing of Jewish immigration on April 24, 1942.) Cuba also lumped Jews with enemy nationals based upon their place of birth. This was positive in a way: Jews were not singled out by religion but by citizenship. As far as Jews are concerned, history gives a black mark to modern Cuba is the affair of the *St. Louis*. 907 Jewish refugees reached Cuba aboard the liner *St. Louis*, on May 15, 1939 and were turned away by island authorities. After much political maneuvering involving the USA, the vessel returned to Europe. Encyclopedia Judaica, Vol. v, p. 1148. This incident was later recounted by Katherine Anne Porter in her novel, Ship of Fools. See also Collie, Tom, "Restoring A Vision," Sun-Sentinel, Florida, August 10, 1997, and American Jewish Historical Society, Ch. 67, "Tragedy of the *St. Louis*," and Tartakower & Grossman, op. cit., p. 90, 120.

Jewry numbered from 12,000 to 15,000, depending upon whose statistics were accepted. According to communal records, the community was 65 percent Eastern European, 25 percent Sephardim and ten percent American. [7]

Several facts about Cuba's Jewish community were significant: this was the largest Jewish population ever concentrated on any Caribbean island; there were more synagogues functioning than ever existed at one time on any island in the West Indies and, the number of Jews in Cuba far exceeded the total amount throughout the West Indies at any one time in its history.

In order to have a clear idea of the full and varied Jewish life then existing in Cuba, one might go to the 1959 edition of World Jewry Today, published on the eve of the upheavals to come from the revolution. The book lists the presence of the following organizations in Havana:

- five active synagogues;
- a chapter of the World Zionist Organization;
- a Jewish Chamber of Commerce;
- a Jewish Women's Association;
- a B'nai Brith Lodge;
- a Club Israel;
- a Hebrew Union;
- a Hapoel Hamizrachi;
- a Zionist organization.

The community supported three schools, of which *Colegio Autonomo de Centro Israelita* was Havana's largest. This school was nationalized after the revolution as a grade school and renamed the Albert Einstein School.

The community also ran a bi-weekly newspaper and an annual publication called *Almanaqaue Hebreo Vida Habanera*. In addition to this flourishing activity focused in Havana, the towns of Matanza, Santa Clara, Camaguey, Santiago de Cuba and Manzanillo all maintained Jewish religious activities.[8]

---

[7] Federbush, Simon, World Jewry Today. T. Yosseloff, N.Y. 1959, p. 418-421.

[8] Postal, B. and Stern, M, op. cit., p. 29.

Jewish life in Cuba reached a peak in 1959 that is as yet unequaled in the Caribbean. Unfortunately, the community became uprooted in the decades of the 1960s and '70s, not through anti-Semitism, but by the politics of the Cuban Revolution. Jewish merchants and businessmen suffered along with the rest of the middle class, which the Revolutionary government systematically destroyed. A new Jewish diaspora began. Just as 300 years earlier, Jews had left Brazil to settle throughout the West Indies, almost all of Cuban Jewry left to enrich Puerto Rico, Miami, New York, Boston and other cities in North and South America.

Some Jews, committed to the Revolution, remained in Cuba and held positions in the new government. They even arranged for broadcasts of Yiddish radio programs, where music, revolutionary propaganda and poems were read. But the greater majority fled. Some even tried to return with the invasion force at the Bay of Pigs in 1960. For this, they spent many years in Cuban prisons.

Interesting Aside:

In 1978, photographer Bill Aron made a trip to Cuba. His photographs were exhibited at the Pucker/Safrai Gallery, together with a 12-page catalogue containing photos and commentary. Aron traveled to Cuba on that government's invitation to visit the Jewish community. Aron's comments "reflect my experiences both on the streets of Havana and with members of the Jewish Community."[9]

What Aron found he detailed in one-half of his catalogue entitled, "The Jewish Community of Havana." The most interesting differences I found from comparing his 1978 photos to current ones, is clothing. In 1978, Jews seem better dressed, wearing suits, ties and fedoras and fashionable dresses. The more recent photos show almost everyone in open-collared sport shirts and plain dresses.

Aron also photographed two cemeteries on the outskirts of Havana. While the community cares for them, they are reported to be deteriorating and are seldom visited.[10]

---

[9] Aron, Bill, Cuba 1978, Pucker/Safrai Gallery, Boston, 1978, un-paginated.

[10] Ramirez, Deborah, 'Judaism Reborn in Cuba," Sunday Sun Sentinel, South Florida Section, August 3, 1997.

In 1978, there were five synagogues in Havana: *Shevet Ahim,* (Sephardic), which still exists; the Union Hebrew Congregation, (Reform) and Cuba's first synagogue, which no longer exists; *Adath Israel* (Orthodox), still in existence; *La Patronata,* the last synagogue constructed before Castro, still in existence and most influential of the remaining synagogues. Another Sephardic synagogue existing in 1987 is now defunct.

Of the once active Jewish life evident from the numbers of synagogues and other communal organizations, only the *Patronata,* once the most influential synagogue in Havana (formed in 1953, shortly before Castro's revolution in 1959) and two other synagogues remain. Yet even these congregations continue to struggle. There has not been a permanent rabbi in Cuba for almost four decades.[11]

Nevertheless, throughout the years the Cuban government has encouraged the continuance of its Jewish community and their synagogues. Jewish communists even attended Passover Seders. And there is no hostility toward Cuban Jews, despite Cuba's lack of relations with Israel and its support of Palestinians since 1973.

Besides ensuring the presence of *matzot* (unleavened bread) for Passover, the Cuban government also allows a kosher butcher to provide meat to the community on a for-profit basis. His was the only free enterprise establishment on the island during the years of

---

[11] "Community's Freedom in Cuba Praised," London Jewish Chronicle. No byline, April 23, 1971. In 1971 while Castro still maintained relations with Israel, the keeping *of kashruth* was permitted with government assistance. There were at that time two ritual slaughterers paid for by the government. To the present time, Jews are permitted a higher ration of kosher meat than the rest of the population. Until recent economic changes in Cuba, the *shochet* (ritual kosherer) was the only free enterprise establishment permitted on the island. For information on kosher food, see Fishkoff, Sue, "A Revolution of Faith," Jerusalem Post, International Edition. October 23, 1993.

its hardline communism. The *shochet* (ritual slaughterer) is also the administrator of the Jewish cemetery.[12]

By 1964, five years after the Revolution, Cuba was still home to the Caribbean's largest community, but it had shrunk dramatically to about 2,586, the majority of whom resided in Havana. In that year, figures compiled by the Zionist Union of Cuba, revealed that the largest age group was between 25 and 60, and that the community was almost evenly divided between men and women.

At the beginning of the 21st Century, there were about 1800 Jews in Cuba, many of them of advanced age and living in Havana, despite the resurgence in other cities. It was the second largest community in the West Indies and beginning to show signs of resurgence. The Jewish community outside Cuba stepped up contact with the island's Jews. And what is equally important, the young Jews of Cuba showed an interest in restoring and maintaining the community. They were active in religious study and resuming religious life in Cuba.

That new interest in Judaism was steadily growing. In 1994, one young man, David Levy, left with Castro's blessings for New York City's Yeshiva University, to study at college and then for the Rabbinate.[13]

Visiting rabbis from Canada, Brazil, Argentina, Mexico and the United States have been performing marriages, conversions, *bar mitzvah* and circumcisions. Prior to their providing these services

---

[12] Ungaro, Joe, "Becoming Cuba's Only Native Born Rabbi," Associated Press, October 13, 1994. Levy was sponsored by New Orleans businessman Barry Katz for his study program. The Cuban community hopes he will return to minister to them. Also, Patron, Eugene, "The Cuban Jews the Rest of the World Forgot," Forward, New York, October 4, 1994. Also, Ramirez, Deborah, "Judaism Reborn in Cuba," Sunday Sun Sentinel, South Florida edition August 3, 1997. Also, Rivera, John, "Cuban Jews Persevere," Baltimore Sun, January 20, 1998. Rivera reports that David Levy expects to return to Cuba. He conducts services during academic breaks while he continues his studies for the rabbinate.

[13] Conversations with and monograph prepared by James and Sue Klau of Temple *Beth Shalom* of San Juan, Puerto Rico, June 2001, and Rabbi Gary Bretton-Granatoor, spiritual leader of Stephen Wise Free Synagogue, New York City, 2000.

beginning several decades ago, these vital rituals had not been conducted, allowing Jewish life to slowly decay.[14]

Lay groups regularly visit the Jewish community, bringing vital pharmaceutical products and food.[15] Medical specialists have assisted the Jewish community in setting up pharmacies and medical clinics. For all this flurry of activity, the community maintains political neutrality, avoiding any position on the government's activities.[16]

Despite official support of the Palestinians, Castro's Cuba has not been repressive of its Jewish citizens. On the contrary, until 1973, Cuba recognized Israel. In that year it became the first government in the Western Hemisphere to recognize the Palestinian Liberation Organization.[17] Yet at home, things did not change for Cuban Jews. As late as 1999, Israeli and Cuban officials arranged for the movement of 600 Cuban Jews to Israel. The Israelis called the movement of newcomers "Operation Cigar." As each new group arrived, immigration officials said they were accepting delivery of 'cigars.' It was understood between Israel and Cuba that there was to be no publicity concerning this arrangement. But newspapers in South America soon discovered what was happening, almost jeopardizing *aliyah*.[18]

Despite all this activity, the community still suffers from its position outside the mainstream of world Jewry, its inability to hire a rabbi because it lacks funds and its loss of the younger generation to *aliyah*. Nevertheless, Cuban Jews maintain a strong

---

[14] Luxner, Larry, "Cuban Jews Wait for a Miracle," San Juan Star, Sunday Magazine, March 28, 1993. Also, Luxner, Larry, "Castro's Jews," National Jewish Monthly, December 1992/January 1993.

[15] Ibid.

[16] Arnold, Michael, "Castro Plays His Jewish Card," Jerusalem Post, October 22, 1999.

[17] Conversations with James and Sue Klau, Temple *Beth Shalom*, San Juan, Puerto Rico, June 2001.

[18] Goering, Lurie, "Cuba's Jews Fight Isolation," Baltimore Sun, Sunday Perspective, August 5, 2001.

will to survive. A Cuba open to the world in terms of politics and free trade seems to be the only hope for them.[19]

Jewish communities outside Havana have also shown resurgence. Defunct for decades, the communities in Santiago and Camaguey have been re-instituted, with establishment of synagogues.[20] Despite there being (a decade ago) only 1,800 Jews on the island, a few hundred less, then, than Puerto Rico (which has the largest Jewish community in the Antilles), Cuba was home to five synagogues: three in Havana and one each in Santiago de Cuba and Camaguey. This was the largest number on any one island in the Caribbean Basin. Despite this activity, Cuba still has no permanent resident rabbi.

Since the 2016 death of Fidel Castro, the leaders of the 1959 Revolution are mostly gone. His brother Raul has taken over the government. President Barack Obama has moved to open Cuba to the United States by allowing more diplomatic ties and cruise ship and airline contact. It is but a matter of time before Jews return to Cuba. How long this will take and in what numbers, only time will tell. This may be complicated by a strong movement of young Cubans who are making *aleyah* to Israel, seriously depleting the numbers of Cuba's Jews.[21].

President Trump has reversed most of President Obama's position on Cuba. That, plus natural disasters in the 21st Century, has led to a further decline in Jewish population. In 2018, it was estimated that there were only 500 Jews living in Cuba.[22]

---

[19] Ramirez, Deborah, "Judaism Reborn in Cuba," Sunday Sun-Sentinel, South Florida edition, August 3, 1997.

[20] Conversations with Cuban historian Martiz Corrales.

[21] "The Last of the Dinosaurs? A Look at Cuba's Dwindling Jewish Community," Jerusalem Post, International Edition, October 14, 2016.

[22] World Population Review, 2020.

The Spanish Caribbean: The Dominican Republic

The Dominican Republic and Haiti share the island of Hispañola, the second largest island in the Caribbean.

Despite an earlier colonial history similar to Cuba and Puerto Rico, the Dominican Republic nevertheless broke away from Spain by its Declaration of Independence in 1844. After a short reconciliation, the Republic achieved final independence in 1865. Caribbean Sephardim, mostly from Curaçao, then settled there.

By 1893, however, they all had been assimilated by this one-time jewel of Spain's West Indian empire. A descendant of that immigrant group was Francisco Henriquez y Carvajal, president of the Dominican Republic in 1916.[1]

The Dominican Republic has a long history of hospitality to Jews. In 1882, General Gregorio Luperón sought unsuccessfully to establish Russian Jews in the Republic as part of an ambitious agricultural program. In the early 1920s another wave of Jewish immigrants came from Eastern Europe and engaged in commerce, unmolested.

By 1938, Rafael Trujillo, the Dominican Republic's dictator, startled the world by opening his country's doors to up to 100,000 Jewish refugees from Europe's hostile political climate. To back up his offer, Trujillo eventually donated almost 55,000 acres of his

---

[1] Arbell, op. cit., p. 47.

own personal land in Sosua, a small northern coastal town near the resort city of Puerto Plata.[2]

It was a time when Europe's Jews were scrambling for friendly havens yet, unbelievably, less than 2,000 accepted this offer.[3] Those who did come built an almost autonomous city with its own school, hospital, synagogue (which was upgraded and a small museum established in 1990,) and even a radio station. Much of this activity was helped by tax waivers for Sosua residents and Jewish agency grants for purchasing livestock, agricultural tools and living quarters.[4]

Despite the disappointingly small numbers who came to the Republic, Trujillo ordered his diplomats to effectuate delivery of about 4,000 Dominican visas to Jews still remaining in Germany. Their possession guaranteed safety from Nazi concentration camps.[5]

But the refugees who did come, most of them German, Austrian and Czechoslovakian, were professionals, civil servants and businessmen who were, not farmers. To them, Sosua was a backwater. The tropical heat, isolation and culture shock worked to discourage colonization. Lack of women in the predominately

---

[2] Postal, B. and Stern, M, op. cit., p. 39. The authors claim Trujillo donated the land. Jack Robertiello, in his article "Dominican Chutzpah, The Story of Sosua," Americas, 1993, states, "Trujillo publically declared the land a gift from the government but he secretly held ownership and was paid." In an anonymous article titled, "Hundreds of Refugees Find Haven in Republic," in the London Jewish Chronicle, June 5, 1958, it was stated that the land was purchased by Trujillo from the United Fruit Company and that it was his personal contribution to the community. There is some evidence to indicate that Trujillo was hoping that Jews would intermarry with Dominicans so that he could "whiten" his race. See Sue Fishkoff's "Trujillo's Jews," Jerusalem Post International Edition, January 25, 1995; Laura Randall's "Golden Cage," Latitudes South, Winter 1995; and an untitled article by Abraham Rabinovich in the Jerusalem Post on December 23, 1965.

[3] Fishkoff, Sue, "Trujillo's Jews," Jersalem Post, International Edition,, January 21, 1995.

[4] Robertiello, Jack, "Dominican Chutzpah: The Story of Sosua."

[5] "Dominican Jewry Undeterred," London Jewish Chronicle, November 19, 1965; Robertiello, Jack, "Dominican Chutzpah: The Story of Sosua."

male colony created dissention. By 1946, more than 600 of their numbers left for the United States and other places.[6]

Those who remained established cooperative agricultural enterprises, including high-grade dairy products and sausage manufacturing. As of this writing, Sosua Jews number less than 150, but their influence is evident: they have made of Sosua a European enclave within a tropical island. Outside cafes serve Viennese and Hungarian treats. Guesthouses are reminiscent of Central Europe. Sosuan Jews quickly integrated into Dominican society; one of their group, Alfredo Rosenzweig, was elected to the Dominican senate.[7]

The reluctance of Jewish immigration to Sosua has puzzled historians, since Jewish agencies actively sought its colonization. To help resettlement of Jewish refugees, the agencies even sent an engineer, Solomon Trone, to Lisbon in 1940 to enlist refugees for Sosua. He could only persuade 100 men to volunteer.[8]

Some contemporary writers claim there were insufficient vessels to transport people. That may be so, but it does not alter

---

[6] Untitled article by Abraham Rabinovich, Jerusalem Post, December 23, 1965.

[7] Postal, B. and Stern, M, op. cit., p. 40.

[8] In a letter titled, "We Didn't Turn our Back," written to the Jerusalem Post, June 7, 1997, Dominican Ambassador to Israel, Alfonso Lockward, disputed an American official's statement that "...no country including the United States..." helped Jews [during World War II]. Lockward verifies that the Republic issued visas to help Jews flee Europe. He then goes on to say, "The size of this program (settlement in Sosua) was reduced due to decisions of the Jewish institutions responsible for its implementation." Lockward points out that as early as 1882, General Gregorio Luperón advised Jewish groups that he would offer refuge to Jews, stating, "the Dominican Republic wants to transform itself into a refuge for all persecuted Jews from other parts of the world." Wischnitzer, op. cit., p. 184, states that when Solomon Trone went to Lisbon to get volunteers for Sosua, he returned with only 100 men. Tartakower and Grossman, op. cit., p. 318, state that the Brookings Institute found the Republic could not accommodate 100,000 refugees as Trujillo had hoped, but only 3,000 to 5,000. The authors dismissed Trujillo's effort as "negligible except for the good example it sets for other nations." But they failed to explain why even the 3,000 to 5,000 refugees figure was never achieved. See also American Jewish Historical Society, chapter 137, "Sousa (sic): An American Jewish Experiment."

the fact that very few sought the refuge offered. Indeed, the history of Jamaica and Trinidad belied the transportation argument. Over 4,000 Jewish refugees were transported to these islands before and during World War II.[9]

Trujillo's unusual concern for Jews did not end with Sosua and the transit visas he issued to German Jews. In 1957, he personally paid for a brand new synagogue for the Jewish community of Santo Domingo, the island's principal city, and had it fitted with luxurious marble and mahogany. In the same year, Trujillo offered Egyptian Jews sanctuary after the Suez Canal War between Israel and Egypt. As a result of that conflict, Egypt dispossessed thousands of its Jews. Once again, Trujillo's offer was not accepted. It should be noted that by this time, the State of Israel was available to absorb most Jewish refugees worldwide.[10]

From 1930 until he was assassinated in 1961, Trujillo was one of the most brutal and cynical dictators in the Western Hemisphere. Despite his reputation as a murderer (he was, among other things, responsible for the massacre of 25,000 Haitians) he nevertheless made good on his promises to the Jewish immigrants. As we shall later see, he financed the Santo Domingo synagogue with his own funds. He was a paradox, of that there is no doubt.

Another point of interest in the Republic concerns Luis de Torres, Columbus' converted interpreter. De Torres' reputation extends beyond Cuba. The tree trunk, to which he moored his boat when he landed in the Dominican Republic, is a museum piece in Santo Domingo's main cathedral. It is in the same place where Columbus' remains are reputed to be resting.[11]

In 1992, The Dominican Republic inaugurated an ambitious monument commemorating Columbus' momentous voyage. Part of the display was dedicated to the Jewish people. A message from Israel's president, Chaim Herzog, states: "The Dominican

---

[9] Postal, B. and Stern, M, op. cit., p 55, 92.

[10] "Hundreds of Refugees Find Haven in Republic," no byline, New York Herald Tribune, June 8, 1958.

[11] Postal, B. and Stern, M, op. cit., p. 41.

Republic... occupies a seat of honor in the memory of the Jewish people and the State of Israel, of which Sosua is an unforgettable symbol."[12]

With communities in both Santo Domingo and Sosua, approximately 350 Jews lived in the Dominican Republic at the beginning of the 21st Century. Less than 50 families make up the Santo Domingo colony, including Israelis in the Dominican Republic on technical aid missions. There is no rabbi, but services are held twice a month.[13] In addition, a Chabad Center has been added to the Dominican Republic, led by Rabbi Shimore Pearlman.

The Jewish community has been losing members for decades, and is estimated by the World Population Review to be at just 100 people in 2020.

---

[12] Robertielli, Jack, "Dominican Chutzpah: The Story of Sosua," Inset in the article by Larry Luxner.

[13] Letter to author from Isaac Rudman, *Centro Israelita*, Santo Domingo.

8

THE FRENCH CARIBBEAN

Martinique

Guadeloupe

Haiti

The French Caribbean:
Martinique & Guadeloupe

The early Spanish and Portuguese settlers on France's West Indian possessions of Martinique and Guadeloupe found these islands less hospitable than the liberal Dutch, English and Danish islands. On the other hand, Jews could expect better treatment from the French than from the Spaniards and their relentless Inquisition.

The French called their Caribbean possessions, *"les isles du vent."* They are located in the Windward Islands about 1,250 miles southeast of Miami, Florida. Before France acquired these islands in 1653, they belonged to Holland. Jews were already living there and already dominating the sugar and cocoa markets. Refugees from Recife, Brazil later joined them in 1654.[1]

When Recifan refugees hopefully presented themselves to the island's Governor for permission to gain entry, Jesuit priests protested vehemently. Permission was never formally granted, but they settled anyway and seem not to have been troubled for lack of authority.[2]

Their influence must have been great, although their numbers were proportionately small. Priests, especially Antoine Biet, constantly complained of a powerful Jewish influence. They pointed out that Saturday, the traditional market day, was

---

[1] Roth, <u>History of the Marranos</u>, p. 290.

[2] Arbell, Mordehay, *"La Istoria de los Sefardis en las Islas de Martinique I Guadeloupe,"* <u>Aki Yerushalayim</u>, #49, 1995, p. 20 (written in Ladino).

changed to Friday to accommodate Jews, so that they could observe their Sabbath. The Jews dominated commerce.

Martinique was not the only French island attracting Recifan refugees. Hundreds, including Jews, went to Guadeloupe and smaller numbers settled in Cayenne on the South American mainland, as French Guyana was then known. By the end of the 1600s, French colonial officials and the clergy were regularly commenting to Paris that much of their island trade was in Jewish hands and that something should be done to curb their influence.

It was in Martinique, however, where Jesuits strongly opposed Jews, their activities and their presence, that colonial policy towards them was shaped. Efforts were made to curb Jewish influence of all sorts. Restrictive laws were passed. But practical island administrators, who were seeking profits and prosperity, largely ignored them. Closing the official eye was to become the colonial government's way of dealing with anti-Jewish laws.[3]

The French islands might have developed strong Jewish communities. But the Jesuits, who exercised strong control over colonial business activities, constantly harassed Jews. Father Antoine Biet noted that Jewish influence was far in excess of the community's numbers.

One special target of the Jesuits was Benjamin d'Acosta de Andrade. He owned two sugar refineries and was the first to process and manufacture cocoa in a French territory. He exported his product to France, calling it chocolate. D'Acosta de Andrade finally left Martinique in despair. Not until 2013, over 300 years later, did the French acknowledge the important contribution made by Sephardim to France's manufacture of traditional fine chocolate.[4]

The Jewish community on the main island of Martinique supported a Sephardic synagogue by 1676. Amsterdam's Spanish

---

[3] Friedman, op. cit., p. 84.

[4] "France Thanks Sephardic Jews for Chocolate 500 Years Too Late," The Times of Israel, May 6, 2013.

and Portuguese congregation lent the congregation one of its *Torahs*, to be used during regular prayers. [5]

Guadeloupe's second largest city, Pointe-à-Pitre, is supposed to have derived its name from an early Jewish refugee from Recife named Pietere, who built a fish-processing plant on that site.[6]

Guadeloupe seems to have had no formal congregation, but there was always constant movement between that island and Martinique, which are close to one other. Sephardim also maintained some presence at Bass-Terre, Guadeloupe's capital.

The champion of a strong and permanent Jewish settlement in *les isles du vent* was Colbert, France's Controller-General. He was able to arrange the 1671 Charter of Liberties, which guaranteed Jewish civil rights. The Crown approved the Charter. But it all came to an end when Colbert died. After much lobbying by the Jesuits, the *Code Noir* (Black Code) was enacted in 1685 and the last positive guarantees that Colbert obtained were lost.

Written primarily as a guide to the conduct of slavery, *Code Noir* also contained provisions that proscribed Jews from settling in French territories. The *Code Noir* promulgated by Louis XIV stated:

> "It is our wish and We decree that the edict of the late King of glorious memory, our greatly honored Lord and father, dated April 23, 1615, be carried into effect in our islands and by those present. We command all our officers to chase out of our islands all Jews who have established their residence there whom as declared enemies of the Christian faith we command to get out in three months counting from the day of the publication of these results upon penalty of confiscation of their persons and property."[7]

---

[5] Arbell, Mordehay, op. cit.

[6] Jewish Communities of the World, p. 45.

[7] Friedman, op. cit., p. 44.

This act was the only formal expulsion order ever issued by a government and directed against Jews in the West Indies.

At first, the decree was ignored, as were earlier anti-Jewish laws But time was running out for the settlers. Discouraged by all the obstacles set before them, Jews began drifting to Dutch, British and Danish islands, to the dismay of administrators charged with overseeing profitable colonies.

Despite the onerous laws, notable exceptions to *Code Noir* were still allowed. The powerful Sephardim of Bordeaux, Bayonne and Marseilles in France were legally permitted to send their sons to the colonies to protect their commercial interests – with government approval. The Gradis family, allied with the Mendes clan, ran six ships from *les isles du vent*. The *Polly, David, Patriarch Abraham, Le Parfait, L'Alliance,* and *Le Vainquer* made regular runs through the islands and to French Canada.[8]

Other families enjoyed similar privileges. They were called *"marchands portugais ou noveaux christiens."* (Portuguese traders or New Christians). Less powerful families were forced to suffer under a series of petty regulations continuously limiting Jewish life and commerce.

The French insistence on making Jewish settlement in its colonies difficult, forced immigration to Dutch, Danish and British islands, where civil status was more certain. Thus, the Nassys, one of the founding families of Surinam Jewry, moved to that Dutch colony from Cayenne, So did the Martinique chocolate exporter and sugar grower, Benjamin d'Acosta de Andrade.

The strength of Jewish communities in French colonies slowly waned. Jews continue to move throughout *les iles de vent*, but sparingly and with caution.

Almost a century after passage of the *Code Noir*, the Crown still refused to give dwindling numbers of Jews living within its territories any legal standing. *Code Noir* was not repealed: the Crown, however, did state for the record that its provisions might be too stringent.[9]

---

[8] Postal, B. and Stern, M, op. cit., p. 78.

[9] Tolkowsky, op. cit., p. 249; also JPP, p. 90.

Following the French Revolution, the civil status of the Jews was to change, both in metropolitan France and within her colonies through the world. It was, unfortunately, too late for the reconstruction of a Jewish community in the French Caribbean. Strong communities and deep roots had long been established in Curaçao, Jamaica, Barbados and other islands. Whatever lure the French West Indies may have possessed had long since vanished, although small groups of unorganized Jews did live in the French Caribbean.

There is a new wave of Jewish migration from France and North Africa bringing Jews to both islands. In 1988, the Orthodox Congregation *Or Sameah* was founded in Pointe-à-Pitre. The 1998 edition of "Jewish Communities of the World," published by the World Jewish Congress, verifies that both Guadeloupe and Martinique are beginning a new chapter in Jewish history for these islands.

Each has a synagogue, a *Talmud Torah* (religious school) and a kosher store. Over 800,000 people live on Guadeloupe and Martinique: of this some 50 Jews live in Guadeloupe and about 400 in Martinique. The members of the Martinique community have created an attractive synagogue, *Talmud Torah* and *mikve* in the suburbs of Fort-de-France. They are led by a Parisian rabbi who belongs to the Chabad movement. This community has created the first synagogue in Martinique in over 300 years.[10]

On a recent visit to Martinique it was noted that a young boy was studying for his Bar Mitzvah. When addressed in French, the lad answered in English, explaining that his parents sent him to school in Miami and he was home for the weekend to study for his Bar Mitzvah.

Even French Guyana has benefited from new immigration. In the early 1990s, a small group of Jews from North Africa and Surinam settled in Cayenne, which is on the north coast of South

---

[10] The Martinique Community maintains a beautiful synagogue in the outskirts of Fort de France, with all the adjuncts necessary for synagogue life; conversations with Elie Ilouz, *parnass* (caretaker) of the synagogue, 2004.

America, and neighbor of Surinam. The Chabad movement assists the approximately 80 Jews of Cayenne.

The 2020 World Population Review lists 900 Jews in residence in Martinique and Guadeloupe.

The French Caribbean:
Haiti

Haiti, lying 700 miles southeast of Miami, Florida, had over eleven-million inhabitants living on its 10,714 square miles in 2018. The first Jew to set foot here was the interpreter Luis de Torres, as he must have done on most, if not all, of the islands discovered by Columbus on his first voyage in 1492.

Haiti is a part of Hispaniola (Little Spain), the name Columbus gave the island. The Spanish ceded Haiti to France in 1697, and the entire island was then known by its French name, *St. Dominique.* Today the island is once again called Hispaniola, but is divided between Haiti, the only independent French-speaking republic in the Americas, and her eastern neighbor, the Spanish-speaking Dominican Republic.

Following the example of their colleagues on Martinique and Guadeloupe, Haiti's colonial administrators did not allow *Code Noir* to materially affect the Jewish population of this French colony.

Throughout the 1700s, Sephardim with names such as De Pas, Sarzedas, Soria and Toussasint owned plantations and traded throughout French Haiti. The Gradis, Mendes and Monsanto families engaged in international trade. The Monsantos maintained family ties in French New Orleans on the North American continent, in St. Thomas, Curaçao and other Caribbean islands. The Sarzedas family later settled in Charleston, South Carolina. Most Jews during this early colonial period, however, seemed to have been in the employ of large plantation owners who came from France and Curaçao.

The Black Revolt of 1790 affected Jews as well as the European colonists. All Europeans were forced to flee Haiti because of anti-white violence. The revolts brought an end to slavery and French domination, creating an independent Haiti. During the insurrection, some Jewish families managed to reach safety in a Haitian town called Jeremie. To this day, many Haitians from Jeremie claim Jewish ancestry.

Some of the Haitian landscape around Jeremie contains names of Jewish interest, attesting to the influence of early Jewish settlers. The town of Jeremie is name for the prophet Jeremiah. There are place names such as *Point-a-Juifs* and *Ause-a-Juifs*. Other influences may be found where Portuguese Jews once lived; their family names such as Moron and Astruc still remain.[1]

Ancestors of former French Prime Minister Pierre Mendes France lived in Jeremie before they moved to Bourdeaux in France. This branch of the renowned Sephardic Mendes family adopted the additional patronymic, France, to distinguish themselves as the Gallic arm of an important and powerful international family.[2]

Abraham and Sara Moises were also refugees from the Black Revolt. In 1791, they went to South Carolina. This couple founded a family that was to enrich American letters and add to the military traditions of the Confederate States of America.

Penina Moises, the daughter of Abraham and Sarah, was the first American woman to publish poetry and literature. Not recognized during her lifetime and unable to earn a living from her literary efforts, Moises nonetheless gained a reputation after her death, both as a poetess and a Jewish activist commenting on Jewish events during the first half of the 19th century.[3]

The rest of the Moises family lived and served in the South with great distinction. Edwin Warren Moises served as an officer

---

[1] Loker, Zvi, "Jewish Typonomies in Haiti," <u>Jewish Social Studies</u>, Vol. X., NY 1978.

[2] Arbell, op. cit., p. 65.

[3] American Jewish Historical Society, chapter 112, "Penina Moises: Day in the Sun."

in the Army of the Confederacy. While an officer in the Civil War, he commanded a company called Moises' Rangers, which was formed in May 1862. It was the only Company officially listed as named for a Jewish officer.[4] After the War, Moises ran for and won the office of Adjutant General of South Carolina.

There is little doubt that the Black Revolt destroyed such Jewish communities as may have existed. Jewish presence in Haiti never regained its vigor.

Before the Black Revolt in the 18th Century, the Jews of Haiti were well-known. On August 18, 1782, members involved in the building of New York's Spanish and Portuguese synagogue wrote to the Jewish community of Cap Francois (now Cap Haitien) for their assistance. At that time, there were about 30 Jewish families in residence. Cap Haitien was then the capital of Haiti.

On another occasion, the American Jew Nephtali Hart appealed for help from his co-religionists in Cap Francois when his brig, the *Elizabeth*, was seized in that port.

Some Syrian Jews immigrated to the capital city of Port-au-Prince following World War I. Eastern Europeans followed. Their numbers were small, and there was much intermarriage, dissolving whatever strength the community may have once had.

During the 1950s and '60s, services were held in the homes of various Jewish leaders. In 1969, the Jewish Yearbook stated that there were 100 Jews in Haiti, and gave a street address near the port for tourists' reference.

Since the political upheavals following the death of the military leader "Papa Doc" Duvalier, however, whatever community there was has been weakened considerably. There is no formally organized Jewish life in Haiti now, although Israel and Haiti enjoy full diplomatic relations.[5]

---

[4] Rosen, Robert, "The Jewish Confederates," Univ. of South Carolina Press, 2000, p. 116, 224- 225, 347.

[5] Jewish Communities of the World, p. 45.

9

The Influence of Caribbean Jewry on Early America

West Indian Sephardim maintained their strength in the Caribbean until the beginning of the 20th Century. In Jamaica and Curaçao, however, they no longer account for most of the Jewish population. Attracted by sugar and plantation economies, these European and Brazilian Sephardim built strong religious communities to which mainland Americans could look to for guidance.

Early Caribbean Sephardim did not usually leave the West Indies. There were families who moved from the Caribbean to New York, Charleston, Savannah and New Orleans, but these were not normal trends. Sephardic Jews already resident in the Caribbean tended to shuttle between islands. When things got bad in St. Eustatius, they left for St. Thomas, St. Martin and Curaçao. If business was slow in Curaçao, they moved to Aruba, St. Thomas or Barbados.

Spanish and Portuguese Jews developed a highly structured and religiously oriented society throughout the Islands. It crossed political boundaries and was designed to perpetuate their cultural heritage, strengthen their religion and keep their families intact. Marriage was encouraged between members of *La Nación*, even to uniting cousins. The strong Jewish communities created in the Caribbean may have been the ideal to which mainland America strived.[1]

---

[1] Karner, op. cit., p. 40-49.

Interesting Aside:

The family structure of colonial Sephardim was highly sophisticated. The purpose basically was to keep the family unit together. This was not limited to Curaçao's Sephardim, but was a feature of all the early Spanish and Portuguese Jews wherever they settled. In 1852, Uriah Phillips Levy married his niece (his sister's daughter), Virginia Lopez. At the time, Levy was 61 and his niece 21. Virginia was born into a wealthy Jamaican family. Her father suffered business reverses and then died after emigrating to New York City. He left Virginia in difficult circumstances. Levy's biographers state, "Uriah undoubtedly married his niece to protect her and give her a home – an act not only permissible by Jewish custom, but considered almost a duty."[2]

When Levy died in 1862, his widow was 28 years old. Under ancient Jewish law, the eldest brother of the widow's husband is obligated to marry the widow. A *chalitzah* is a release of this obligation. Jonas Phillips Levy, Uriah's brother, performed this ritual release. Thus, Virginia Lopez Levy, who died in 1925 at the age of 90, had been free to marry any man of her choice.[3]

In fact, Libo and Howe in their book, We Lived Here, Too, make the point about American Jews that, "In the history of the United States as a nation, these early Jewish settlers have only a modest importance. We can all remember from our school years the stories about Jewish merchants supplying Washington's hard-pressed armies; perhaps we may also remember that he had a loyal adjutant who was also Jewish. But you could write a respectable history of the United States in the 17th and 18th centuries without giving more than a few paragraphs to the Jews. The Jews scattered across the colonies had no communal organization binding them from Georgia to New England."[4]

---

[2] Fitzpatrick and Saphire, Navy Maverick: Uriah Phillips Levy, p. 196.

[3] Sharfman, The First Rabbi, p. 263; see also pages 308-312 for detailed discussion on *chalitzah*.

[4] Libo and Howe, We Lived There, Too, p. 20.

The strong structural organization and wide influence of Caribbean Jews lacking in continental America, ran to every element of Jewish society in the West Indies. The fact that young men left an island to seek business opportunities elsewhere did not mean that family or community ties were severed. These emigrants formed satellite colonies of their home island.

In any marriage outside the religion, it was expected that the Jewish parent would raise the children within Judaism and that a Christian wife would convert. This ideal was not always achieved. As a result, Jews and Catholics with the same family name exist side-by-side as family units throughout the Caribbean, Venezuela and Colombia.[5]

Because of this and other structured rules, Spanish and Portuguese Jews of the Caribbean maintained their cultural identity into the 20th century. Indeed, Jamaica, Curaçao and Surinam can still point to descendants of original settlers among their Jewish population.

Settlers on the American mainland did not construct such elaborate social rules, and very few Sephardim who trace their lineage to early colonial America have escaped assimilation or intermarriage.[6]

It may also be that early West Indian Spanish and Portuguese Jews, many of whom were only a generation or so away from the Inquisition and the Recife diaspora, were well aware of the need to maintain their religion. They were determined to practice and nurture Judaism to the greatest extent possible. The political climate of the Caribbean went a long way to helping them to do so.

In 1678, Barbados was a community less than 30 years old, with 300 souls, yet they brought a rabbi from Amsterdam to minister to them. They had built and prayed in a synagogue even before their rabbi arrived. Less than a century after its founding, tiny Barbados had two synagogues.

---

[5] Karner, op. cit., p. 44.

[6] Roth, History of the Marranos, p. 290.

The St. Eustatius community built its synagogue less than 20 years after its beginning and enjoyed the ministry of two rabbis between 1775 and 1790.

Curaçao summoned its first rabbi, Josiao Pardo (the first in the West Indies and North America)[7] and built its original religious structure in 1675, just 20 years after its first significant settlement. Two other synagogues were built as the congregation grew; the first in 1692 and another in 1703.

Jamaica followed the same pattern. Curaçao's rabbi, Josiao Pardo, moved to Jamaica in 1683. A synagogue already existed on this island at Port Royal.[8]

And when the Jews of St. Eustatius moved to St. Thomas in 1796, they did a characteristic thing: they almost immediately built a synagogue. By 1833, they had built several on the same spot, to replace those damaged by fire and hurricane.

Compare this to mainland colonial America. Although also founded in 1654 by refugees from the Recife diaspora, New York's first Spanish and Portuguese synagogue was not erected until 1729, 75 years later. The Sephardic ritual was maintained in New York although by this time Ashkenazim outnumbered Sephardim. A second synagogue was not built in the city of New York until 1825.[9]

Philadelphia's first permanent Jewish settlement dates back to 1737, although small pockets of Jews lived there before then. A rented building that was used as a synagogue dates back to 1761. Not until 1782 was Philadelphia Jewry to consecrate its own building. No American city had two synagogues functioning concurrently until 1802, when *Rodeph Shalom* opened its doors in Philadelphia. The city's Jewish population at that time may have been under 500.[10]

---

[7] Emmanuel, I. and S., <u>A History of the Jews of the Netherlands Antilles</u>, p. 518-519.

[8] De Souza, E. <u>Pictorial: Featuring Some Aspects of Jamaican Jewry</u>, p. 11; Silverman, B, United Congregation of Israelites.

[9] Grinstein, op. cit., p. 32.

[10] Scharfman, <u>The First Rabbi</u>, p. 143-146.

Jewish literature of early America is filled with depressing descriptions of negative religious conditions besetting mainland Jews. Their lack of religious observance, violations of religious obligations and other problems were regularly documented in the Jewish press and in letters between religious leaders.

One must look hard to find similar problems in the Caribbean although assuredly there were some. The only serious issues that seem to have arisen were the way some West Indian rabbis performed their services, as modernization or liberalization of some services created dissention within a community, Rabbi Benjamin Cohen Carillion of St. Thomas wanted to change the order of his service, confirm girls and add Reform practices to the Sephardic ritual in the early 1800s. He had to leave St. Thomas.[11]

Although there were learned Jews in the United States, many of whom had studied for the rabbinate in Europe, no ordained rabbi had a congregation in any American synagogue until 1840.[12]

In 1772, Rabbi Haim Carigal had preached in Spanish and Ladino to the Newport, Rhode Island congregation, yet was not offered a pulpit. Congregation member Aaron Lopez and his family, lately from Spain, could have welcomed a Spanish-speaking rabbi. In 1772, Lopez was one of the wealthiest Jews in the American colonies.[13]

In 1840, Rabbi Abram Reiss, who later changed his name to Abraham Rice, migrated from Bavaria to become the first ordained rabbi with a congregation in the United States. He took a pulpit in Baltimore, a city at that time with only 200 Jewish families.[14]

The United States was then home to 15,000 Jews, half of whom were resident in New York City. It took another five years for America's second ordained rabbi to come to the United States.

---

[11] Paiewonsky, Isador, Jewish Historical Development in the Virgin Islands 1655-1959.

[12] Scharfman, op. cit., p. 74.

[13] Friedman, Lee M., Rabbi Haim Isaac Carigal, Boston, 1940 (privately printed) p. 14. Also, American Jewish Historical Society, "How Hebrew Came to Yale."

[14] Scharfman, op. cit., p. 81.

Synagogues of the West Indies, however, were at this time regularly attended by rabbis. They had no trouble finding pulpits throughout the Caribbean. As we have seen, Rabbi Josiao Pardo moved from Curaçao to Jamaica. St. Thomas' rabbi, Benjamin Cohen Carillon, after antagonizing his congregation, left there to lead another Jamaican synagogue at Montego Bay. Other West Indian rabbis tended to remain with their congregations for long periods, perhaps because they were part of the island family. The extreme examples are Rabbi David Cardoze and Moses Sasso. Between them, they logged 101 of continuous service in St. Thomas, beginning in 1864 and ending with Rabbi Sasso's retirement in 1965.[15]

Rabbi Meir A. Cohen Belifante serviced Barbados from 1730 to 1752, his office ending upon his death. Jamaica and Curaçao had similar experiences.[16]

Caribbean congregations were also sending rabbis to the United States mainland on a regular basis. Abraham Pereira Mendes, the Jamaican rabbi who succeeded Rabbi Carillon at Montego Bay, saw his two sons, Henry and Frederick, go on to become outstanding American rabbis. Frederick Pereira Mendes served at *Shaarey Tefillah* in New York for 47 years, until 1920. He was also on the editorial board of the Jewish Publication Society and an editor of the Jewish Encyclopedia. Henry Pereira Mendes was *hazzan* and later rabbi, at New York's Spanish and Portuguese Synagogue from 1877 to 1923. He was one of the founders of the Union of Orthodox Congregations of America and a staunch Zionist. Abraham, their father, had his final pulpit at Newport, Rhode Island.[17]

Other religious leaders have come to the United States from Surinam and Curaçao. Religious leaders also made the move from the United States to better opportunities in the Caribbean. In 1736,

---

[15] Jewish Historical Development in the Virgin Islands, 1655-1959. See entries for 1869 and 1914. Also, Libo and Howe, op. cit., p. 21.

[16] Shilstone, op. cit., pp. 141-143.

[17] De Souza, Pictorial: Some Aspects of Jamaican Jewry, p. 19.

Moses López Da Fonseca, *hazzan* at New York's Spanish and Portuguese Synagogue, moved to Curaçao.

Thus, from 1654 until 1840, the only ordained rabbis in the Western Hemisphere held pulpits in the West Indies and Surinam. Perhaps no North American congregation could afford a rabbi; maybe rabbis did not wish to live on the American frontier or in some wilderness community. But during those years, Philadelphia, New York and Charleston were certainly cities of culture and amenities at least equal to the Caribbean.

There may be another, more practical reason for Caribbean Jewry's fervor in maintaining their religion. All islands were isolated and the Europeans on them were greatly outnumbered by slaves. Often, early European populations were no more than a few thousand, with slaves from four to five times their numbers. Under such conditions, it was logical for Jews to look to their religious institutions to satisfy social needs. Unlike mainland Jews, who lived in larger population centers with easy access to the other cities and greater social opportunities, West Indian Jewry lacked such options. The synagogue, its school and adult study were probably the only social outlets for Jews. For while they maintained good business and other relations with their Christian neighbors, house visiting and other close socializing between Christians and Jews were not common in early island societies.

Another area of influence Caribbean Jews exerted on the mainland was in trade. Mainland American mercantile houses doing business with the Caribbean had clerks who spoke Spanish and Portuguese. In addition to using these languages in their synagogues, Sephardim used them between themselves, at home and in business. In order to take advantage of the lucrative Caribbean trade with Sephardim, American counting houses had to be proficient in these languages.

Even visiting rabbis, who preached in American synagogues, did so in Spanish. Haim Carigal, the well-known rabbi from Palestine who finally settled in Barbados, traveled from Palestine to the Caribbean and the American mainland. He preached as a guest minister at the Newport Synagogue, in Spanish, in 1773. Carigal was a great influence on Ezra Stiles, President of Yale

University. Through Carigal, Stiles was impelled to add Hebrew to Yale's curriculum.[18]

So the power and prestige of Caribbean Jews was formidable during the two centuries following the Recife diaspora. They erected synagogues, employed rabbis, were active and important in North American trade. They kept the Jewish religion alive and vital in the dark periods following the Expulsion from the Iberian Peninsula.

Their contributions do not end there. All the rights we take for granted now and accept as part of our heritage as citizens of the Western Hemisphere, did not come without a struggle, for which we must remember the Jews of the Caribbean. For during this period Colonial [American] Jews were steadily subject to the threat of disenfranchisement at the whim of colonial authorities who, in day-to-day affairs, pretty much held all the power in their hands. One can speak of the liberality of spirit in the Colonies only with some discounts and qualifications.

"As they came here [the colonial American mainland] the Jews must have been struck by the fact that some of the leading political figures, those soon to become the founding fathers of the Young Republic, were espousing a doctrine of universal liberty and religious toleration. This doctrine was of course violated in practice, as all such doctrines are: Negroes were enslaved and Jews and Catholics suffered discrimination in several colonies."[19]

The Caribbean Jews worked hard as early civil rights activists. They became property owners and assumed the burden of serving in island militias. They used their influence to secure personal and religious liberties for all Jews in the New World, by insisting on their right to vote, hold religious services, erect synagogues and pray in them. They led the way for us all.

---

[18] Friedman, Lee M., op. cit., p. 2.

[19] Libo and Howe, op. cit, p. 33.

10

The Jewish Caribbean: Today and Tomorrow

In an article appearing on September 18, 1970 in The Jewish Post and Opinion, headlined, "Slow Demise Seen for Caribbean Jewry," a grim future was predicted for the Western Hemisphere's oldest Jewish communities.

In 1969, riots broke out in Curaçao which, while not anti-Semitic, caused heavy damage to the Jewish community. At the same time, Black Power activists caused concern not only for Jews but all Caucasians in Trinidad and other islands.

The passage of three decades has proven the article wrong. Jamaica and Curaçao have seen assimilation and movement of its young people to the United States and Europe, but those remaining are aware of their heritage and work hard to perpetuate it. The reality of Jewish life in the Caribbean is that it ebbs and flows with good and bad economic times.

Since the writing of that article, extensive restorations of historic structures have taken place in Surinam, Barbados and Nevis. Such work was later undertaken in St. Thomas and St. Eustatius. All this activity is jointly Jewish and governmental. There is a deep understanding of the Jewish presence and its contribution in the West Indies, not only by Jews, but also by non-Jews. Much of the restoration work could not have been done without the assistance of private and government help and funds; the local Jewish population does much of the actual work.

The community of St. Croix enlarged with the acquisition of its own building. A small Jewish community has taken root in Sint Maarten. St. Thomas is strong and shows no sign of weakening.

151

Puerto Rico, the Caribbean's largest community, continued strong after having suffered losses due to economic changes, most of which saw American clothing and shoe manufacturers leaving the island to seek cheaper labor elsewhere. Both the Reform, Chabad, and Conservative congregations have strengthened and are definitely institutions that will continue well into this 21st century. The addition of the Chabad Learning Center in the late 20th Century made Puerto Rico the only island with representatives in all major branches of Judaism.

At the writing of the article in 1970, the Jewish community of Santo Domingo was smaller than it was in later years.

One must remember that even at their peaks, Caribbean Jewish communities were relatively small. Curaçao's community was probably never greater than 2,000 at its most influential. Compare that to Cuba's 12,000 in 1960.

While Cuban Jews continue to struggle, as does the rest of the island, the community is awakening. The synagogues of Santiago de Cuba and Camaguey have reopened; a young Cuban has gone to New York to study at Yeshiva and he hopes to return to Havana to minister to the Jews of that city.

For the first time in almost 300 years, the island of Martinique is home to a Jewish community with a synagogue, *mikveh*, school and rabbi. A Chabad Center was established in the early 2000s.

In order to realize the impact of Jews in the Caribbean, one must understand the region's history. There were never more Caucasians than Africans on any island with a plantation economy. Since slaves had no influence in the social and commercial life of an island, Jewish influence was particularly strong, especially when they represented 25-50% of all Europeans. Upon slavery's abolition, Caucasians were immediately a political minority on any island: reduced to three to five percent of the overall population.

True, the decline of Sephardic families able to trace their ancestry to the Recife diaspora has been steady. But Sephardim have disappeared in most regions worldwide, where they once were influential. In the Caribbean, there is an awareness of their antecedents among non-Jewish families who have intermarried with the Sephardim. They take pride in their roots. These are feelings one rarely finds elsewhere except, perhaps, in Spain. These descendants have contributed to the life of the region both culturally and politically.

Jews from Russia, Poland, the United States and other places have taken the place of the old Spanish and Portuguese families. They have instilled new vigor into old communities. Yet, as stated previously, economic hardship and natural disasters have a great influence on the size and establishment of Jewish communities in the West Indies. Between 2017 and 2020, natural disasters have severely affected the Jewish population: many islands took years to recover from one fierce hurricane before another struck. Then, a devastating earthquake was followed by the world-wide Coronavirus pandemic. History tells us that the Caribbean region has undergone dramatic changes before, but rebounds nevertheless.

The future should bode well for Caribbean Jewry. The power the Castros exert over an exhausted Cuba will soon come to an end. There is no reason to doubt that a free and enterprising Cuba will again attract Jews. Perhaps Cuba will regain its once numerous community, perhaps not, but it will certainly rise again to add vitality to Jewish life in the West Indies.

Additionally, one of the most important and significant factors dominating Jewish life in the Caribbean is the Chabad movement. At this writing, there are 15 Chabad Learning Centers throughout the Caribbean archipelago. Every Jewish community (except Surinam) boasts a Chabad Center led by a rabbi and his wife who have become fixtures in Jewish community life.[1]

---

[1] World Jewish Congress.

Chabad Learning Centers in the Caribbean

1. Puerto Rico
2. U.S. Virgin Islands
3. Dominican Republic
4. Netherland Antilles
5. Martinique
6. Cayman Islands
7. Aruba
8. Jamaica
9. Grenada
10. St. Barth
11. Curacao
12. Bahamas
13. St. Lucia
14. Turks & Caicos
15. Barbados

11

Epilogue

On July 15, 1834, the Queen Mother Maria Christina of Spain abolished the Spanish Inquisition. For 363 years it had spread malevolence against anything other than Roman Catholic orthodoxy. And despite its end, the centuries had laid down a layer of inhospitability to non-Catholics that continued for decades afterwards. Only when Spain lost Cuba and Puerto Rico to the United States in 1898 did Jews feel they could settle on these Hispanic islands.

But Spain did eventually throw off its anti-Semitic attitudes. By World War I, a small Jewish colony had grown in Spain. The government was aware of its existence, but chose to ignore it. By 1932, Spain's prime minister, Primo de Rivera, sponsored legislation that encouraged the return of Sephardic Jews to that country; a Sephardic Law of Return. During World War II, Primo de Rivera's law saved some European Sephardim who were granted Spanish protection from Nazi concentration camps.

Portugal, too, was neutral during that War and both were minimally hospitable to Jewish refugees, granting them asylum until they could arrange for passage to safe havens.

By the 1960s, Jews were openly praying in synagogues all over the Iberian Peninsula, from Lisbon to Madrid and Marbella to Barcelona. The wheel came full circle when King Juan Carlos of Spain, openly sympathetic to the Jews of his country, attended a Madrid synagogue in 1992, wearing the traditional *keppah* (skullcap) on his head.

155

In 1992, Spain and the Jewish people were fully reconciled. The events of 1492 and the long period of alienation between them were over, as Spain's 500 year observation, *"Sepharad '92,"* celebrated Sephardic Jewry.

In 2007, Spain and Portugal both sponsored citizenship legislation, encouraging the return of descendants of the expelled Jews of 1492 and the forcibly converted Jews of Portugal of 1497. As of this writing, 10,000 persons in Turkey, Israel and the U.S. have taken advantage of the laws.

It is expected that the Jews of Spain and Portugal may once again restore the term *Sepharad* to its original brilliance.

1

Overview of
Jewish Caribbean Settlements

2

Historic Synagogues and
Cemeteries in the Caribbean

3

Jewish Communities Not
Historically Associated with the
Spanish & Portuguese Jews

Appendix 1:
Overview of Jewish Caribbean Settlements

Surinam		
Year	Settled By	Last Jewish Presence
1536	Secret Portuguese Jews, English, then Dutch Sephardim, 1639-1652, followed by French and Italian Sephardim. Central European Jews followed in the 1700s.	Jews still live there. It is the oldest permanent Jewish community in the Western Hemisphere and remains active.

Aruba		
Year	Settled By	Last Jewish Presence
1563	First settlers were unknown secret Jews.	
1754	Later, Dutch Sephardim. Not significant until early 20th century. Then, Balkan, Central European and Dutch Jews settled here.	Jews still live here, with an active community.

St. Maartin		
Year	By Settled By	Last Jewish Presence
1791	Refugees from St. Eustatius.	
20th Century	Dutch Sephardim; Dutch Jews of the Caribbean, United States and Jews of Central Europe.	Small community at present.

Curaçao		
Year	Settled By	Last Jewish Presence
1651	Dutch Sephardim; regular migrations from other Caribbean islands, Holland, Turkey and Europe for four centuries. At one time, the largest and most powerful Jewish community in the New World.	Active Sephardic and Ashkenazic community still exists.

St. Eustatius		
Year	Settled By	Last Jewish Presence
1722	Dutch and English Sephardim. European Ashkenazim. The center of trade in the Northern Hemisphere until the end of the American Revolution.	Last Jews left in 1850.

Jamaica		
Year	Settled By	Last Jewish Presence
16th Century	First settled by secret Spanish Jews. Conquered by England in 1655; Jews came into the open. Sephardic and later European Jews settled here. Once England's greatest New World colony, Jews played an important role in Jamaican history.	Jews still active. Sephardim and Ashkenazim hold services together.

Barbados

Year	Settled By	Last Jewish Presence
1654	Settled by Recifan Jews who were Dutch Sephardim. Later settled by English Sephardim and other Jews of the Caribbean. Important in the development of sugar, rum and molasses. Community disappeared early in the 20th century.	Small congregation of American, English and Canadians.
1930s	European, English United States and Canadian Jews returned.	

Nevis

Year	Settled By	Last Jewish Presence
1684	English and Dutch Sephardim.	No Jews at present.

Trinidad-Tobago

Year	Settled By	Last Jewish Presence
16th Century	Secret Spanish Jews lived here during Spain's occupation. England took possession in 1818. Caribbean Sephardim and later English and European Jews settled here in 20th Century.	Small unorganized community.

St. Thomas

Year	Settled By	Last Jewish Presence
1634	Small initial settlement of Sephardim from Recife.	
1791	Sephardim from St. Eustatius.	
20th Century	Third wave from U.S.	Strong active community.

St. Croix

Year	Settled By	Last Jewish Presence
1760	French	Small community.

Puerto Rico

Year	Settled By	Last Jewish Presence
1898	Some secret Jews lived here during Spanish rule. Not until 1898 when U.S. took over from Spain did Jews openly settle. Mostly U.S. Ashkenazim and Cubans. Jews from Europe and Asia followed.	Three active communities, Conservative, Reform and Chabad.

Cuba

Year	Settled By	Last Jewish Presence
1898	Secret Jews lived here but no formal settlement until 1898. First U.S. Jews and Curacaoans came. Then Europeans Sephardim and Ashkenazim migrated. Once by far the largest Jewish community in the history of the West Indies (15,000) it is now second to Puerto Rico with approximately 500	Active community.

Dominican Republic

Year	Settled By	Last Jewish Presence
1865	Sephardim from Curaçao, Venezuela and Columbia.	
1939	European refugee colony in Sosua	Small groups in Santo Domingo and Sosua

Martinique & Guadeloupe		
Year	Settled By	Last Jewish Presence
1654	Dutch Sephardim, refugees from Recife. All Jews were expelled from French possessions in the New World in 1685. While there have been sporadic Jewish communities, none have been permanent or significant until recently.	
1990s	Chabad community; Orthodox	Organized community

Haiti		
Year	Settled By	Last Jewish Presence
17th Century	Settled by Dutch and French Sephardim who left during so-called, "Black Revolt."	
20th Century	Syrian and European Jews, who left in 1970s and '80s during political unrest.	No significant Jewish presence

Appendix 2:
Historic Synagogues and Cemeteries
in the Caribbean

Often, writers have made contradictory and erroneous claims about which Jewish community, synagogue or cemetery is the oldest in the Americas. To set confusion aside, I researched the origins of every known synagogue and cemetery in the West Indies. Written records for this region being what they are, dates can often only be approximated. Wherever possible, I used dates set by the communities themselves. I believe them to be more accurate than other sources, since the communities are the custodians of their own records.

Cemeteries are more difficult to document than synagogues. The gravestones of early settlers were often made of soft materials, which have since crumbled, the dust blown away. The assaults of constant heat, humidity, sun and *salitre*, the sea salt in the air that is peculiar to the islands have, over the centuries, combined to wear down the remaining stones, often making them illegible.

Because one cemetery may contain older gravestones than another, it does not necessarily testify to its antiquity. It may only prove that some stones have greater durability, and surviving markers are the starting points with which we try to determine a cemetery's age. It should be remembered that Recife, which predates all Jewish settlements in the Western Hemisphere (1630-1654) also had two cemeteries. There are no surviving stones of which we are aware, since the Portuguese erased all traces of the Jewish community upon recapturing Recife.

Curaçao, one of the largest and most important repositories of 17th, 18th, and 19th Century headstones and monuments in the Americas, sustained serious damage from the fumes of the island's oil refineries. Other cemeteries also suffer from the effects of modern pollutants, such as hydrocarbons, industrial soot, coal particles and sulfuric acid. Caribbean cemeteries are in constant danger of being overgrown by vegetation, the tropical sun, the *salitre* in the air and by neglect.

Barbados may once have had five different cemetery sites, one of which was dedicated to the burial of suicides and Christian spouses. They have been lost to posterity. At present, only three sites remain. Many of the remaining stones are broken, the result of earthquakes and other natural causes.

The cemeteries of Surinam, Jamaica and the older St. Thomas plot at Savan are subject to constant encroachment by heavy tropical foliage, making them inaccessible and prone to serious deterioration. Attempts have been made in the past to clear the cemeteries, but the tropical climate and its vegetation always reclaims the land from the cemeteries.

Here, then, based on the current state of information and my own personal investigations, is a listing of the known historic synagogues and cemeteries extant in the West Indies. They are all deserving of preservation as monuments of a unique and fascinating community in Jewish history, the first in the New World. If they are not saved, they may be lost forever.

Surinam

Synagogue: *Beracha Ve Shalom*
Constructed: 1685
Location: 35 miles southwest of the main city of Paramaribo, in the area known as the *Joden Savanne.*

Presently in the jungle and overgrown with thick vegetation, it is the oldest synagogue structure still standing in the Western Hemisphere, and may probably be the first in the Caribbean.

Located in the overgrown *Joden Savanne*, two cemeteries belonging to the original settlers of the oldest continuous Jewish community in the New World lay beneath a heavy tropical tangle. The cemeteries have been cleared of brush several times in the past decades, but have again been reclaimed by the jungle.

Synagogue: *Tzedek V Shalom*
Constructed: 1736
Location: Paramaribo

Tzedek V Shalom no longer exists as a synagogue in Surinam; it has a new life in Israel. After a dwindling community could no longer support two synagogues, *Tzedek V Shalom* sat idle. In 1999, the Jewish Museum of Israel negotiated with the government of Surinam for the entire contents of the synagogue. It is considered a "long-term loan." The building still stands in Surinam, devoid of its religious effects.

Tzedek V Shalom was classical Caribbean Sephardic, with a second story woman's gallery and sand on the floors. It was the second synagogue Jews living in rural *Joden Savanne* built when they began settling in the city of Paramaribo.

Surinam

Synagogue: *Neve Shalom*
Constructed: 1734
Location: Paramaribo

The original Sephardic synagogue of Paramaribo was constructed on a plot donated by the Dutch government after the residents of the *Joden Savanne* began experiencing an exodus to the city. Jews used the old *Baracha Ve Shalom* with less frequency. When Sephardim and Ashkenazim fell to quarreling in the first decades of the 1700s, it ended in a settlement that ceded *Neve Shalom* to the Ashkenazim. The new owners made a promise to continue using the Sephardic ritual. That promise has been kept. The entire Jewish community of Paramaribo, Ashkenazim and Sephardim alike pray at this synagogue. The community was fortunate to have a dynamic representative, René Fernandes who, in 1992, planned an ambitious ceremony on the 500th anniversary of the Spanish Expulsion.

Nevis

Synagogue: **Name unrecorded**
Constructed: 1684?
Location: Charlestown

It was thought that a two-story building constructed of brick, now reduced to a single level, may have been at one time the Nevis synagogue. That has proved to be false, although it is still known among islanders as The Jews' School. This may be the building in which the Revolutionary patriot Alexander Hamilton received his early education – including the study of the Hebrew language.

The Georgetown cemetery in Nevis was once overgrown, as are many other historic Caribbean cemeteries. This site was restored in 1971 through the efforts of Rabbi Malcolm Stern and Robert and Florence Abrams (who maintained a winter home in Nevis.) The old graveyard was re-consecrated on February 25, 1972.

This writer was present to observe the importance the island government ascribed to the event. The Prime Minister and other notables attended and spoke at length of the significance of the Jewish presence in Nevis' history.

A stone wall and iron gate were erected to surround the restored site. Rabbi Malcolm Stern was able to decipher 17 stones and part of an 18th. The earliest stone dates back to 1684 and belongs to Batsheba Abundiente.

See the section in Nevis in this book for a listing of the stones in this cemetery. New archeological findings have discovered additional graves which have no headstones. The government of Nevis maintains the cemetery in excellent condition to this day.

St. Eustatius

Synagogue: *Honen Dalim*
Constructed: 1734
Location: Oranjastad

The street upon which the synagogue ruins still stand is called, Jews Way. The island government does its best to maintain the structure (which is now only the remaining outer walls and a stairway to a long lost second floor, in good condition.). It has even erected a well maintained, whitewashed picket fence around the old synagogue.

In Orangestad, about half a mile from the ruins of *Honen Dalim*, the old cemetery in St. Eustatius is notable for several reasons. Of all the burial places where a Jewish community no longer exists, this is the only one that has never been overgrown by vegetation. The people of St. Eustatius have, to their credit, traditionally taken care of the gravestones. They have also raised money to replace the synagogue's crumbling walls and have plans to restore a roof.

The graveyard and stones are in good condition, compared to other gravesites I have seen in the Caribbean. Two fine iron gates surround the cemetery, with metal work depiction of the Ten Commandments and the year of the cemetery's consecration, 1739, worked into them.

The earliest decipherable grave is dated 1742 and belongs to Abraham Hisquiau de la Motta, who died May 10 of that year. Twenty-one legible gravestones are contained here.

Another interesting feature is the cistern nearby, which is purported to have been the community's *mikvah*. Piping extends from water accumulated in the trough of an extinct volcano leading to this facility.

Sint Maarten

Synagogue: **Name undocumented**
Constructed: circa 1783
Location: Philipsburg, Aacherstratt

The Jewish community of Sint Maarten petitioned Dutch authorities for permission to build a house of worship in 1783. It is not certain that the ruins in back of the now extinct West Indian Tavern on Aacherstratt are actually those of the synagogue. They are on the spot where a synagogue was once located. All that remains are part of a brick wall. By 1828, there were reports that the building had fallen to ruin.

Although no formal evidence exists of a Jewish cemetery on this island, whatever proof can be mustered arises from some facts that are known: In Philipsburg, on the far end of Aacherstratt (Front Street) where the synagogue was constructed, a plot of land was acquired for a cemetery. Some childrens' graves, believe to have been those of Jewish youths, have been found in this area and the path along this area is still called, Jewish Cemetery Alley.

Curaçao

Synagogue: *Mikve-Israel*
Constructed: 1732
Location: Willemstad

The oldest synagogue structure in the Americas (1732) still offers regular religious services. Originally following the Sephardic ritual of the Spanish and Portuguese, with those languages incorporated in its service. In 1964, *Mikve Israel* merged with Temple *Emanuel,* a Reform congregation, and adopted the Reconstructionist ritual. The synagogue maintains a Jewish museum and a restored *mikvah*.

This distinguished congregation was the premier congregation of the Americas, "Queen Mother of the Caribbean."

Curaçao

Synagogue:	*Temple Emanuel*
Constructed:	1864
Location:	Willemstad

This structure is no longer used as a synagogue. It still stands in the city and is regularly used as a meeting place. The land on which it stands was donated by the Dutch government. Temple *Emanuel* is the Caribbean's first Reform synagogue.

The most famous Jewish cemetery in the Caribbean is located at Blenheim. Its oldest gravestone is dated 1668 and belongs to Jeudith Nunes de Fonseca. (It is not, however, the oldest continuously used Jewish cemetery in the Americas for which we have records. That distinction belongs to Barbados, whose first recorded grave dates to 1660.)

Threatened with deterioration by Shell Oil refinery fumes during the years following World War II, the community worked to prevent further ravaging with the application of protective chemicals.

It is a wealth of knowledge for historians and an interesting collection of beautifully sculpted marble depicting a deceased life's work and other religious scenes. It is estimated that there are between 5,200 and 5,500 graves at this site. Unfortunately, less than half have decipherable inscriptions.

At Berg Altena, a newer cemetery opened in 1864 and is in current use.

Barbados

Synagogue: *Nidhe Israel*
Constructed: 1833
Location: Bridgetown

There was always a synagogue on the site of *Nidhe Israel* (the first c. 1679) on Synagogue Lane. The present synagogue is a faithful restoration of one that itself was built in 1833, replacing another wrecked in a hurricane. Funds for the present restoration were raised through private subscription by Jews throughout the world.

The building had not been used as a synagogue since 1929, when it was sold to an entrepreneur. Fifty-eight years later, on December 18, 1987, the newly re-consecrated synagogue was once again open for Jewish prayers.

Three cemeteries flank the path leading directly to the synagogue in Bridgetown. Synagogue and cemeteries are all contained within a walled compound just off Synagogue Lane and Magazine Lane.

As the visitor enters the gate, there is a sign on the stone wall on Synagogue Lane advising Cohens (who, by Jewish law, are not permitted contact with the dead) that they may avoid passing the graveyards by using the back entrance.

There may have originally been a series of five separate graveyards in the compound, including one for suicides and Christian spouses. Only three sites now remain.

The earliest burial is documented in the year 1660, which gives Barbados the oldest Jewish cemetery in continuous use in the Americas; 12 years earlier than Jamaica and eight years before Curaçao. The stone belongs to Aaron de Mercado and is catalogued as tombstone No. 230, in Eustace Shilstone's well-known work on the Barbados cemeteries.

The tiny Jewish community of Barbados (about 60 adults) is presently restoring the cemeteries, which contain many broken and undecipherable stones.

173

St. Thomas, U.S.V.I.

Synagogue: ***Beracha V'Shalom***
Constructed: 1833
Location: Charlotte Amalie

Beracha V'Shalom is the oldest synagogue in continuous use under the American flag. The oldest synagogue structure in the United States is the Touro Synagogue in Newport, Rhode Island, constructed in 1795, 38 years before *Beracha V'Shaolom*. However, for at least three periods during its history, Touro Synagogue was used for purposes other than a house of worship. It currently offers services to an established congregation.

St. Thomas' two cemeteries, Savan, located on the outskirts of Charlotte Amalie and Altona, in Charlotte Amalie, are each filled with history of the Caribbean and the world. Here are the remains of David Levy Yulee's family. Yulee was the first Jew to sit in the U.S. Senate. Also, the family of Camille Pissarro is interred here. Pissarro, the world famous Impressionist, was born in St. Thomas.

Savan, the older of the two, has over the years become overgrown. The cover of this book shows Rabbi Joseph Karasic walking the old cemetery in 1971. He and I spent that warm day beneath the tropical sun, armed with machetes of the type used by sugarcane cutters, chopping away the tropical tangle to reveal historic stones. But the persistent underbrush reclaimed the cemetery shortly thereafter.

The Hebrew dates on the wrought-iron gate correspond to 1749-1835. The St. Thomas congregation has undertaken to restore and clean up Savan, as it does Altona, which has the distinction of being both historic and in current use.

Altona is located just outside the town of Charlotte Amalie. The community cleans this area on a regular basis. I would often walk through the cemetery on my frequent visits to St. Thomas. Recently, however, the community felt it necessary to lock the entry gate. On my last visit I was unable to go in because the keeper of the keys was off the island.

Altona dates from the close of Savan to the present time. Other cemeteries, of the Moravians and other religions, surround it. Even if you cannot gain entry, you can look through the gate and over the wall to get an idea of what Caribbean cemeteries look like.

See also Margolinsky's "299 Epitaphs on the Jewish Community in St. Thomas, W.II. 1837-1916"; I. Paiewonky's Jewish Historical Development in the Virgin Islands, particularly the entry under 1957 for cemetery notes; the Bulletin of the St. Thomas Jewish Congregation for April 1994, which contains information regarding volunteer groups cleaning up both Altona and Savan. Among some of the implements the volunteers were told to bring were, "Clorox, laundry soap, gallons of water (per grave), rags, drinking water and gloves (optional)."

Those who could not attend could sponsor an alternate for $25. It is interesting to note that the Altona Cemetery "Grave Wash", as it was called, mentioned that the stones "are quite dark from airborne dust and pollution."

Jamaica

Synagogue: *Shaare Shalom* (also known as the Duke Street Synagogue and the United Congregation of Israelites)
Constructed: 1885
Location: Kingston

This synagogue is the last of the historic classical Sephardic style synagogues built in the Caribbean. It was damaged by earthquake and fire in 1907 and repaired. In 1911, the Ashkenazi community joined with the Sephardim, thus the name, United Congregation of Israelites. *Shaare Shalom* still offers services. It has abandoned the Sephardic ritual in favor of the English Liberal Service, similar to Reform.

Jamaica

Synagogue: ***Beth Yankakob***
Constructed: 1844
Location: Montego Bay

This congregation had an interesting history. From this place, the Periera Mendeses, father and two sons, all rabbis, were to enrich American Jewry with their presence. A flight of stone steps is the only remains of the wooden synagogue that was destroyed in 1912 by a storm.

Jamaica is notable because of the many cemeteries existing throughout the island. The most significant of the cemeteries and the first one established in Jamaica is located at Hunts Bay, Kingston. It's earliest legible stone is dated 1672 and belongs to Abraham Izidro Gabay. In 1968, the Jamaica National Heritage Trust assumed ownership of the treasure in order to preserve it. Unfortunately, the cemetery has fallen into disuse. In addition to Hunts Bay, other cemeteries exist in Kingston, one on Orange Street and the other on Elleston Road.

Historic Jewish cemeteries exist in Sav-La-Mar, Lucea, Falmouth, Brown's Town, St. Ann's Bay, Port Maria, Alligator Pond, Manchester, Morant Bay, St. Thomas, Lacovia, St. Elizabeth, Luistead, Annotto Bay, Old Harbour and Montego Bay. Many have only a handful of stones.

Jamaicans have been in the habit of transferring graves from these smaller cemeteries to larger sites in Kingston, making even the newer ones interesting from an historical standpoint.

No other Caribbean island has the historic wealth of grave locations as Jamaica.

Jamaica

Synagogue: *Neveh Shalom*
Constructed: 1704
Location: Spanish Town – Kingston

This synagogue was constructed in 1704 after the infamous earthquake that destroyed the city of Port Royal and its one synagogue. Remains of *Neveh Shalom* still exist.

St. Croix, U.S.V.I.

Synagogue: **Unknown**
Constructed: 18th – 19th Century
Location: Christiansted

Located in the suburbs of Christiansted, a small Jewish cemetery of a few graves is all that remains to remind us of this short-lived community. The first grave is dated 1779 and the last, 1862.

Aruba

Synagogue: *Beth Israel*
Constructed: 1962
Location: Oranjestad

In 1992, the Jewish community in Oranjestad cleaned up the small cemetery on Boerhavenstraat. Mrs. Martha E. Lichtenstein, secretary of the Board of Directors of *Beth Israel* of Aruba, reminded us in a letter dated June 17, 1993, that it "the only landmark of Jewish presence in past centuries." Rabbi I. Emmanauel, author of <u>History of the Jews of the Netherlands Antilles,</u> copied only two epitaphs in 1940. They are dated 1857 and 1883. There were only a few other nameless graves, he reported.

Bahamas

Synagogue: **Unknown**
Constructed: 19th Century
Location: Nassau

In a walled section of the public section of the Nassau cemetery, there are stones of 19th century English Sephardim.

Appendix 3:
Caribbean Jewish Communities
Not Historically Associated
with the Spanish and Portuguese Jews

For a region with relatively few Jews, the West Indies has many communities scattered from Cuba to Surinam. Here is a list of known Jewish communities throughout the region that have no historic connections with the early Spanish and Portuguese settlements.

Cuba

- *Shevet Ahim*: founded 1914, Sephardic, Havana
- *Adath Isrtael*: founded 1925, Orthodox, Havana
- *La Patronata*: founded 1953, Conservative, Havana

Closed during the 1980s was the Reform Hebrew Union Congregation, Cuba's first synagogue founded in 1904, and *Beth El*, another Sephardic congregation.

Two congregations have reopened: *Union Israelita de Oriente* is in Santiago de Cuba and *Centro Israelita de Camaguey* is in Camaguey.

Dominican Republic

- *Sosua Jewish Congregation*, founded 1940, Orthodox, Sosua.
- *Centro Israelita*, founded 1956, Orthodox, Santo Domingo.

Puerto Rico

- *Shaare Tzedek*, founded 1954, Conservative, San Juan.
- *Beth Shalom*, founded 1967, Reform, San Juan.
- *Chabad* Learning Center, founded 1999, Ultra-Orthodox, San Juan.

Sint Maartin

- Small Jewish community in Phillipsburg, no building, no affiliation.

Martinique

- *Cong. Kanef Haaretz*, synagogue consecrated 1997, Sephardic Orthodox, Fort de France.

Martinique and Guadeloupe are the 3rd and 4th Sephardic Orthodox congregations founded in the 20th Century; the first two were founded in Cuba.

Guadeloupe

- *Cong. Or Sameah,* founded 1988, Sephardic Orthodox, Pointe-à-Pitre.

Aruba

- *Cong. Beth Israel*, founded 1962, Liberal, Oranjasted.

Barbados

- *Shaare Tzedek* synagogue consecrated 1969, Conservative, Bridgetown. (Congregation existed prior to that date without permanent synagogue.) This is the congregation that restored *Nidhe Israel* (1832), which they use during the winter.

- *Congregation of Zion*, founded 1976, Orthodox, Bridgetown.

Curaçao

- *Shaare Tzedek*, founded 1926, synagogue consecrated 1959, Orthodox, Willemstad.

St. Croix

- *Bnai Or*, founded 1978, unaffiliated, Fredrikstad.

Bahamas

- Bahamas Jewish Congregation, founded 1996, Reform, Nassau.

- Freeport Jewish Congregation (*Luis de Torres* Synagogue), founded 1970, Reform, Freeport.

Bibliography
Books & Articles

Aaron, Bill, Cuba, 1978. Pucker/Safari Gallery Catalogue Exhibit, Boston, 1978 (photographs with titled explanations).

A Brief History of the Jewish Settlement in Barbados. Barbados Board of Tourism, Bridgetown. Undated, c. before 1987

"A Brief Synopsis of the Barbados Jewish Community," Bulletin, Barbados Jewish Community, November, 1991

Acosta, Velarde, Federico, El Primer Tribunal Supremo de Pujerto Rico, San Juan, PR, 1940 (Booklet reprint of series of articles appearing in Spanish in El Mundo, San Juan 1940)

Algazi, Julio, "Pontes Istorikos," Aki Yerushalayim, Kol Israel, Jerusalem, #156, 1997. Written in Ladino.

American Jewish Experience from 1654 to the Present, Museum of American Jewish History, Philadelphia, 1981

American Jewish Historical Society. Beginning in 1997, the AJHS began inserting historical articles in the weekly newspaper, The Forward, NY. Some were numbered; others were not. We cite those that are pertinent to this week, as follows: AJHS, chapter # if available, and title.

Amler, Janet Frances, Christopher Columbus' Jewish Roots, Jason Aronson, New Jersey, 1992

Arbell, Mordehay, "Daniel Levi de Berrios, Poeta, dramaturgo i istoriador," Aki Yerushalayim, Kol Israel, Jerusalem #15, special ed. Written in Ladino.

Arbell, Mordehay, "*La istoria de los Sefaradis en las islas de Martinique i Guadeloupe,*" Aki Yerushalayim, Kol Israel, Jerusalem, January, 1999. Written in Ladino.

Arbell, Mordechai, The Spanish and Portuguese Jews in the Postage Stamps, *Semana*, Jerusalem, 1992

Arbell, Mordehay, "Surinam," Aki Yerushalyaim, Kol Israel, Jerusalem #46, 1992. Written in Ladino.

"Archeologists to Excavate Jewish Site in Caribbean," The Reporter, Binghamton, New York, December 9, 1993 (no byline)

Arnold, Michael, "Castro Plays His Jewish Card," Jerusalem Post, October 22, 1999

Arrieta,R., "*Boricuas de Adopcion,*" El Nuevo Dia, San Juan, Puerto Rico, Feb. 12, 1996. Written in Spanish.

Barlew, Rahel Bakish, "*La Komunidad Djudia de Bordeauzx,*" Aki Yerushalayim, Kol Israel, Jerusalem, January 1999. Written in Ladino.

Bercker, Avi (ed.) Jewish Communities of the World, Institute of World Jewish Congress, Jerusalem, 1999

Berkey, Barry and Velma, "Jewish Presence in Aruba," Washington Jewish Week, District of Columbia, December 17, 1998

Bodian, Miriam, Hebrews of the Portuguese Nation, Indiana University Press, 1999

Bogen, David S. "Mathias de Sousa: Maryland's First Colonist of African Descent," Maryland Historical Magazine, Baltimore, Spring 2001

Boyd, Ellsworth, "Hamilton's Roots: Letter from Nevis," Forward, New York, March 19, 1999

Brooks, A.A., "A Jungle Journey," Reform Judaism, N.Y., Spring 1999

"Charlestown Synagogue Excavation": Nevis Field Studies Centre, 1996 (press release)

Cohen, Martin (ed.), Sephardim in the Americas, American Jewish Archives, Waltham, MA, 1992

Cohen, Robert, Early Caribbean Jewry: A Demographic Perspective, Jewish Social Studies Quarterly Journal, N.Y. 1983

"Community's Freedom in Cuba Praised," London Jewish Chronicle, April 23, 1971 (no byline)

De Souza, Ernest Henriques, Pictorial: Featuring Some Aspects of Jamaican Jewry, Kingston, Jamaica (privately printed) 1986

"Dominican Jewry Undeterred," London Jewish Chronicle, November 19, 1965 (no byline)

Donovan, F. & Saphire, S., Navy Maverick: Uriah Phillips Levy, Doubleday & Co., NY, 1963

Dubiez, F.J., The Sephardic Community of Amsterdam, Holland (no publisher, no date, un-paginated, translated from the Dutch.)

Emmanuel, Isaac and Suzanne A., History of the Jews of the Netherlands Antilles, 2 Vols, American Jewish Archives, Waltham, MA., 1962

Emmanujel, Isaac, Precious Stones of the Jews of Curaçao: Curaçaoan Jewry 1656-1957, Block Pub. Co., N.Y., 1957.

Encylopedia Judaica, Jerusalem, 1978 edition

Evans, Eli N., Judah P. Benjamin: The Jewish Confederate, MacMillan, New York, 1998

Ezratty, Barbara T., <u>Puerto Rico Changing Flags 1898-1950</u>, Omni Arts, Baltimore MD. 1986

Ezratty, Barbara T., <u>Puerto Rico: An Oral History 1898-2008</u>, Read Street Publishing, Baltimore MD. 2009

Ezratty, Harry A., "Jewish Heritage in the West Indies," <u>Caribbean Beachcomber</u>, San Juan, P.R., March/April 1969

Ezratty, Harry A., *"Kommemorasion En Statia,"* <u>*Aki Yerushalayim*</u>, Kol Israel, Jerusalem, #48, 1993. Written in Ladino.

Ezratty, Harry A., *"Las Sefardis De Nevis,"* <u>*Aki Yerushalayim*</u>, Kol Israel, Jerusalem, #50, 1994. Written in Ladino.

Ezratty, Harry A., "Old Sephardic Cemetery Reconsecrated in Nevis," <u>Journal of Sephardic Studies</u>, Vol. V., Yeshiva University, New York, 1971

Ezratty, Harry A., <u>They Led the Way: The Creators of Jewish America</u>, Omni Arts, Baltimore, MD. 1999

Ezratty, Harry A., "When Spain Rescued Jews from Hitler," <u>Jewish Digest</u>, N.Y. 1962

Farah, Douglas, "The Ruins of Jewish Savannah," *The Washington Post*, October 31, 1997

Federbush, S., World <u>Jewry Today</u>, T. Yoseloff, N.Y. 1959

Fishkoff, Sue, "A Revolution of Faith," <u>Jerusalem Post</u> Int'l Edition, October 23, 1993

Fishkoff, Sue, "Trujillo's Jews," <u>Jerusalem Post</u>, January 21, 1995

Fovil, Faith, "Bahamas Jewish Congregation: Experience a Sense of 'Kehilah'," <u>Nassau Guardian</u>, October 10, 1997

Fovil, Faith, "Bahamas Jewish Congregation Celebrates First Bar Mitzvah," <u>Nassau Guardian</u>, 1999

French, A.W., "In a Surinam Jumble: The Quest for Identity," New York Times International Ed., October 23, 1999

Friedman, Lee M., Jewish Pioneers and Patriots, Jewish Publication Society, Philadelphia, 1955

Friedman, Lee M., Pilgrims in a New World, Jewish Publication Society, Philadelphia, 1948

Friedman, Lee M., Rabbi Haim Isaac Carigal, Boston, 1940 (privately printed)

Gilbert, Martin, Sir, Jewish History Atlas, MacMillan, London, 1969

Grinstein, Hyman, B., The Rise of the Jewish Community of New York 1654-1860, Jewish Publication Society, Philadelphia, 1947

Harrison, Donald H., "Jews in Puerto Rico," San Diego Press Heritage, March 16, 2001

Hartog, Dr. J., History of Sint Maarten and St. Martin, Jaycees of Sint Maaraten, Philipsburg (undated)

"History of the First Jewish Settlers in Aruba," Bulletin of Beth Israel of Aruba, c. 1993

Hooker, Bernard (ed.), The United Congregation of Israelites, Kingston, Jamaica (undated)

Hooker, Bernard, "Pulpit in the Sun," London Jewish Chronicle, (c. 1968)

Huisman, Piet, Sephardim: The Spirit That Has Withstood The Times, Netherlands, 1984

"Hundreds of Refugees Find Haven in Republic," New York Herald Tribune, June 5, 1958 (no byline)

"Interim Chief of State Installed in Panama," New York Times, April 8, 1964 (no byline)

Jane, Cecil, (translator), Journal of Christopher Columbus, Bramhall House, New York, 1960

Karner, Frances P., The Sephardics of Curaçao, Assen, The Netherlands, 1969

Kayserling, Dr. M., Christopher Columbus and the Participation of the Jews in the Spanish and Portuguese Discoveries. Herman Press, N.Y., 1968

La Nacion: The Spanish & Portuguese Jews in the Caribbean, Beth Haatefutsoth, Tel Aviv, 1981

"La Nacion: Los Judios Españoles y Portugueses en el Caribe," State Dept. of the Commonwealth of Puerto Rico, 1992

Lewin, Boleslaro, "The Crypto Jews who Colonized Brazil," (translation) Jewish Digest, New York November 1970. Original in Spanish published in Revista Conservadora del Presiamento Centroameriano, Vol. 15, #471, August 1966, Manuaga, Nicaragua

Libo, Kenneth and Howe, Irving, We Lived There Too, St. Martin's Press, N.Y. 1984

Lockwood, A. , "We Didn't Turn Our Back," (letter written to the Jerusalem Post, published Oct. 22, 1997, by the Dominican Ambassador to Israel.)

Loker, Avi, "Jewish Toponomics in Haiti," Jewish Social Studies Quarterly Journal, N.Y. 1978

Luxner, Larry, "Castro's Jews," Jewish Monthly, Dec. 1992/Jan. 1993

Luxner, Larry, "Cuban Jews Wait for a Miracle," San Juan Star, March 28, 1993

Luxner, Larry, "Reclaiming Joden Savanne," Americas, 1994

Luxner, Larry, "Tropical Sanctuary," National Monthly, July/Aug 1994

Marcus, Jacob Rader, Memoirs of American Jews, (3 vol.) Jewish Publication Society, 1955

Marcus, Jacob Rader (ed.), American Jewry: Documents 18th Century, Hebrew Univ. College, Cincinnati, 1959

Margolinsksy, Julius (editor), 299 Epitaphs in the Jewish Cemetery in St. Thomas, W.I., Copenhagen, 1965

Marsden-Smedley, Hester, "The Jews of Nevis," London Jewish Chronicle, August. 15, 1969

Maslin, Simon J. (ed.), Synagogue Guidebook, Curaçao, 1964

Maslin, Simon J., "The Omen," Reform Judaism, New York, Winter 2000

Michener, James, The Eagle and the Raven, T. Douherty, N.Y. 1990

Millis, Walter, The Material Spirit. Literary Guild of America, N.Y. 1931

Morales Carrion, Arturo, Puerto Rico: A Political and Cultural History, W.W. Norton, N.Y. 1983

"Nevis Building May Have Been Jewish Temple," Associated Press, September 11, 1993 (no byline)

"Our 'Snoa', 5492-5742," Cong. Mikve Israel-Emanuel, Curaçao, N.A. 1982

Paiewonsky, Isidor, Jewish Historical Development in the Virgin Islands 1655-1959, St. Thomas, 1959

Patron, Eugene, "The Cuban Jews the Rest of the World Forgot," Forward, February 4, 1994

Perry, Dan, "Congregation Shrinks at Historic Synagogue," Associated Press, May 2, 1999

Postal, B. and Stern, M., Tourists Guide to the Jewish History of the Caribbean, American Airlines, N.Y. (undated, c. 1974)

Rabinovich, Abraham, article in Jerusalem Post, no title, no date

Ramirez, Deborah, "Judaism Reborn in Cuba," Florida Sun-Sentinel, August 3, 1997

Randall, Laura, "Golden Cage," Latitudes South, 1995

Relkin, Stanley T. and Abrams, Monty R. (editors), A Short History of the Hebrew Congregation of St. Thomas, St. Thomas, U.S.V.I. 1983

"Return to Toledo: An Overview of Abraham Zacuto, Mapmaker to Columbus and Vasco de Gama," Congress Monthly, September/October 1992

Rivera, John, "Cuban Jews Persevere," Baltimore Sun, January 20, 1998

Robertiello, Jack, "Dominican Chutzpah," Americas, 1993

Rolnick, Josh, "Jewish Paradise in the Caribbean?" Moment, August, 2001

Rosen, Robert, The Jewish Confederates, Univ. of South Carolina Press, 2000

Rohter, Larry, "A Brazilian City Resurrects its Buried Jewish Past," New York Times Int'l Edition, May 19, 2000

Roth, Cecil, A History of the Marranos, Jewish Publication Society, 1959

Roth, Cecil, The Spanish Inquisition, W.W. Norton, New York, ed. 1996

Sacher, Harry, Farewell *España*, Vantage Books, New York, 1994

Saul, Moshe, *"Pirates I Korsarios Djudios,"* Aki Yerushalymim, Kol Israel, Jerusalem, #62, 2000. Written in Ladino.

Saxon, Lyle, Laffite the Pirate, Pelican Press, Gretna (reprint) 1996

Schappes, Morris U. (ed.), History of the Jews in the U.S. 1654-1875, Citadel Press, N.Y. 1950

Scharfman, Harold I.,The First Rabbi, Pangloss Press, N.Y. 1988

Serviss, Naomi, "Reclaiming Jewish Past in Nevis," Latitudes, 1998

Shilstone, Eustace, Monumental Inscriptions in the Burial Ground of the Jewish Synagogue at Bridgetown, Barbados, Jewish Historical Society of England, London, 1958

Silverman, H.P., "Jamaica Blends Ancient and Modern Judaism," London Jewish Chronicle, (date unknown)

"Spain and the Jews," Diplomatic Information Service, Spain, 1949

"Spain Grants Recognition to Haham," Jewish Chronical, London, August 15, 1969 (no byline)

Staub, M., "Puerto Rican Jews: A Cultural Melange," Florida Sun-Sentinel, May 1, 1998

Stern, Rabbi Malcolm, A List of the Tombstones in the Jew's Burial Ground, Nevis, 1971

Stinte, E.A., "Jews had Big Role in Life of Barbados," Bridgetown, Barbados (publication and date unknown)

Strouse, S. S., "He Learned Hebrew from Tombstone Inscriptions," Jewish Digest, New York, July 1970

"Statia's Historic Salute," Information Bulletin of the Government of St. Eustatius

Sturhan, Joan, Carvalho: Portrait of a Forgotten American, Richwood Pub. Co., New York, 1976

Surinam Jewish Community Bulletin, Paramaribo, April, 1991

"Surinam to Join Caribbean Community," San Juan Star, May 26, 1993 (no byline)

Swart, Ken, "Near Doom," Florida Sun-Sentinel, date unknown

Tartakower & Grossman, The Jewish Refugee, Institute of Jewish Affairs, American Jewish Congress and World Jewish Congress, N.Y. 1944

Tollkowsky, Samuel, They Took to the Sea, T. Yoseloff, N.Y. 1964

Tiuchman, Barbara, The First Salute, Ballantine Books, N.Y. 1988

"Two Hundred Fifty Attend Sedarim in Havana," London Jewish Chronicle, April 18, 1969

Ungaro, Joe, "Becoming Cuba's Only Native-Born Rabbi," Associated Press, February 13, 1994

"Welcome to Congregation Beth Israel: The Jewish Community of Aruba," Bulletin of the Aruba Jewish Community, Sept. 2000

Williams, Eric, From Columbus to Castro, MacMillan, New York 1970

Wischnitzer, Mark, Visas to Freedom: The History of HIAS, World Publication Company, Cleveland, 1956

Woods, Edith de Johngh, The Royal Three Quarters of the Town of Charlotte Amalie, MapesMonde, U.S.V.I., 1992

Additional Sources

Altman, Paul. Leader of Jewish community of Barbados, Conversations with

Berkovitz, Edward and Jane, "Memoirs of Sint Maarten, NB.A. 1971-1985

Beth Israel Community Bulletin, Aruba, 1993 and 1999

Bradshaw, Hon. R.L., Prime Minister, St. Christopher, Nevis. Address at Re-consecration Ceremonies of the Jew's Burial Ground, Nevis, W.I., February 25, 1971,

Bretton-Granatoor, Rabbi Gary, spiritual leader of the Stephen Wise Free Synagogue, New York City, regarding mission to Cuba 2000.

Bronstein, Alan, president of Congregation B'nai Or, St. Croix, U.S.V.I... Conversations with

Corcos, Salatiel Negrón, President of Temple Beth Shalom, San Juan, P.R., Correspondence with, June 2020

Davis, Michael, secretary, K.K. Nidche Israel, Barbados, W.I. Conversations with

De Souza, Rev. Ernest, United Congregation of Israelites, Jamaica, W.I., Correspondence with

Esfakis, Suzanne Jaffe, resident of Nassau, Bahamas, Conversations with

Fernandes, René, President of Sephardic Community, Surinam. Letter to the author together with additional materials supplied and set forth in this bibliography

Forward, a weekly New York newspaper has been publishing articles submitted by the American Jewish Historical Society of Waltham, MA. since 1997. These articles pertain to American Jewish history. Most are numbered in consecutive order. We list the articles as AJHS, with their titles and chapter numbers, if available.

Grynzstein, I., Cong. *Shaare Tzedek*, Curaçao, N.A. Correspondence with

Hayman, Jay, Rabbi of the St.Thomas Synagogue, *Beracha V'Shalom*. Conversations with

Ilouz, Elie, *parnas* of Cong. *Kenaf Haaretz*, Martinique, F. W. I., Conversations with

Klau, Sue and Jim, Temple *Beth Shalom*, San Juan, Puerto Rico. Conversations and material regarding mission to Cuba, 2001.

Lichenstein, Mrs. Martha F., *Beth Israel* Synagogue, Aruba, W.I., Correspondence and conversations with

McAllister, Gay, Historian, St. Eustatius, N.A. Conversations with

Morales, Hiram, Temple *Beth Shalom*, San Juan, P.R., Conversations with and materials supplied about Carlos Roloff of Cuba.

Newsletters of Bahamas Jewish Congregation:

| 13-Jan-1997 | 24-Apr-1997 | 12-May-1997 | 18-Jul-1997 |
| 28-Jul-1997 | 21-Aug-1997 | 28-Dec-1998 | 23-Jan-1999 |

Newsletters of the St. Thomas Jewish *Congregation Beracha V'Shalom*, April 1994 and March 1994

Oran, Marshal, President, K.K. *Nidche Israel*, Barbados, W.I. Conversations with

Paiewonsky, Isador. Address titled "300 Years of Jewish Culture," March 23, 1973, St. Thomas, U.S.V.I.

Rudman, Isaac, *Parroquia Israelita, La Republica Dominicana*, Dominican Republic. Correspondence with

St. Maarten National Heritage Bulletin, showing floor plans of the supposed synagogue and possible *mikvah*.

Surinam Jewish Community Bulletin, Paramaribo, April, 1991

Tattersall, Jill. Correspondence regarding Jewish community in Tortola, British Virgin Island

Zeitlin, Prof. R. N., Brandeis University. Letters and conversations 1993-1995

Index

C

D

ABOUT THE AUTHOR

Harry A. Ezratty is an attorney by profession, specializing in Admiralty Law. He is a graduate of New York University and Brooklyn Law School. His avocation is his Sephardic heritage. For over 45 years he has studied, researched, written, and taught about the history of Spanish and Portuguese Jews throughout the world.

Ezratty lived in the Caribbean for more than 35 years and visited most of the islands of the West Indies. During his continuing travels, he seeks out abandoned and existing Jewish sites, prays in Caribbean synagogues and collects pertinent documents, photographs, and the folklore of island Jews.

He has written extensively and lectured on the topic throughout the Caribbean and the United States. 500 Years in the Jewish Caribbean gathers all this material in one interesting volume, which covers the history of Caribbean Jews and their impact on the Western Hemisphere, particularly the United States, which is further explored in the companion volumes, They Led the Way: The Creators of Jewish America, and The Builders: Jews and the Growth of America.

Mr. Ezratty presently resides in Baltimore, Maryland.

CPSIA information can be obtained
at www.ICGtesting.com
Printed in the USA
LVHW021813130721
692589LV00012B/1126

9 780942 929492